WINDOWS to HEAVEN

WINDOWS to HEAVEN

Introducing Icons to Protestants and Catholics

ELIZABETH ZELENSKY

& LELA GILBERT

Brazos Press
Grand Rapids, Michigan

Published by Brazos Press
a division of Baker Publishing Group
P.O. Box 6287, Grand Rapids, MI 49516-6287
www.brazospress.com

Printed in the United States of America

Unless otherwise marked, Scripture quotations are taken from the HOLY BIBLE, NEW INTERNATIONAL VERSION®. NIV®. Copyright © 1973, 1978, 1984 by International Bible Society. Used by permission of Zondervan. All rights reserved.

Scripture quotations marked KJV are taken from the King James Version of the Bible.

Library of Congress Cataloging-in-Publication Data
Zelensky, Elizabeth
    Windows to heaven : introducing icons to Protestants and Catholics / Elizabeth Zelensky and Lela Gilbert.
        p.   cm.
    Includes bibliographical references.
    ISBN 1-58743-109-2 (pbk.)
    1. Icons. 2. Orthodox Eastern Church—Doctrines. I. Gilbert, Lela. II. Title.
BX378.5.Z45 2005
246'.53—dc22   2004020352

For our families, especially our sons Paul Zelensky and Dylan Gilbert, in whose friendship lay the beginning of this book.

Special thanks from Lela to Howard and Roberta, who introduced me to Byzantium, and sincere gratitude from both Lela and Elizabeth to Chad Allen for his grace, kindness, and professionalism.

"Beauty is truth, truth beauty."

John Keats

Contents

Introduction: Seeing and Believing   9

1. Salvation in Words and Images   19
2. Andrei Rublev's Icon of the Holy Trinity   37
3. The Vladimir Theotokos   55
4. Theophanes' Transfiguration of Christ   71
5. The Dormition of the Virgin   91
6. The Sinai Pantocrator   103
7. The Church: Where God Dwells among Men   123

Epilogue   139

Introduction

Seeing and Believing

I appeal to you, brothers, in the name of our Lord Jesus Christ, that all of you agree with one another so that there may be no divisions among you and that you may be perfectly united in mind and thought.

—1 Corinthians 1:10

One warm summer Sunday, Anne glanced out the front window of her New England house and noticed that the Russian Orthodox church across the street was surrounded by displays of Russian handcrafts and that a tent had been set up, apparently as a small cafe. The Sunday service was over, and dozens of people were milling around. She could hear their voices; they were speaking both Russian and English.

9

A sign was posted saying "Russian Festival—Welcome!" so she walked across the street and up the path to the church. Its golden domes gleamed in the sunlight, the smell of food was inviting, and all around her people were purchasing Russian Christmas ornaments, handcrafts, baby clothing, and small Orthodox icons.

Anne stopped to look at the various items for sale and was especially curious about the icons, which were beautifully detailed with gold and brilliant colors. She wondered vaguely what they were for but was interrupted by some girls from the neighborhood who wanted her to join them for a snack in the food tent.

Later, as she was about to return to her home, she noticed that the door to the church was ajar. Curious, she pulled it open and peeked inside. The large sanctuary, dimly lit by only a few windows, was aglow with candlelight. As her eyes adjusted, Anne saw a screen of icons at the front of the church, gleaming with gold. There were no chairs or pews, and here and there candles surrounded other large icons similar to the small ones she had seen outside.

Of course Anne recognized Mary and the infant Jesus, and she recognized images of Jesus as an adult. But there were other images—some bearded old men, for example, wearing robes adorned with crosses—that were unfamiliar to her. In front of several of the icons were vases of informally arranged garden flowers. The scent of roses blended with that of incense lingering from the service.

Anne wasn't sure what everything meant, but there was a feeling of space and beauty in the sanctuary. The silent church with its candlelit icons filled her with a profound sense of peace. I wish I were Russian, she thought. I think I'd like to come to church here.

10

Henry Fulton, pastor of a large evangelical church in Southern California, had just returned from a trip to Greece and Turkey and was welcoming his elderly aunt and uncle to lunch at his home. He was showing them a book of photographs of the trip, which included a visit to an ancient monastery in Greece. "Oh, that reminds me," he said, "let me show you something else."

He left the room and returned with an icon he had purchased at the monastery. About 8 × 12 inches, it was a reproduction of the face of Christ, his head surrounded by a golden halo, his serious eyes fixed on the viewer.

"Look at this," he said, handing it to his aunt. "Isn't it beautiful?"

Henry's aunt, who was a German immigrant in her midsixties, stared at the image for a moment and then abruptly handed it back to him. "I don't like this at all," she said firmly.

"You don't like it?" Henry was puzzled.

"No, I've never approved of those things," she said, and her husband nodded in agreement.

"Approved of them?" Henry repeated. "What do you mean?"

"Well, you know they are worshiped as idols . . ." she said.

"Oh, but that's not true at all," Henry exclaimed. "Orthodox Christians don't worship idols! That's very

11

clear if you read the writings of some of the early church fathers."

The woman paused only for a moment. "Well, you know more about all that history than I do," she said, "but those idols, or icons, or whatever you call them still look weird to me. I think they are scary. Even if they aren't really idols, there's just something about them that scares me."

Visiting an art museum in the Midwest for the first time, a history professor was eager to see the art and artifacts on display there. She was Christian and was especially interested in a collection of Orthodox icons on loan from a Greek museum. Understanding the complexities of the collection, she had given herself ample time to move through the galleries, to absorb its more subtle aspects, including its historical roots.

In one gallery, she found herself face to face with a medieval icon of St. Peter. Although she was well versed in art history, she had never seen this particular image before. She stopped in her tracks and stared at the face, which seemed to stand out from all the rest. Was it the colors that had caught her attention? It was not an opulent icon, gleaming with rich gold highlights or rimmed in pearls. It was far more subtle than that, predominantly green and accented with touches of ochre.

More than anything else, it was the face that drew her— peaceful, meek, and humble. It differed from many of the other icons in its modesty. She found a nearby bench and sat down, still staring. Unexpectedly, a wave of emotion *swept across her mind, bringing tears to her eyes. She took a deep breath and suddenly felt as if she were in church. Her mind was silenced, and the peace of the icon quieted her spirit. It was a sacred feeling, even though she was in a thoroughly secular environment.*

Why? she asked herself as she finally rose to leave. It seemed as if the icon had a mysterious voice of its own, speaking peace to her, reminding her of other realms and realities. Was such a thing possible?

"Seeing is believing." That's what we say when we express a preference for the concrete over the intangible. From Show and Tell in elementary school to "Missouri, the Show Me State," sight is the key element of our empirical Western worldview.

Paradoxically, Eastern Orthodox Christians use this same sense of sight for a dramatically different purpose—to access the realm of transcendence, the dwelling place of Eternal Beauty and Truth, through the contemplation of stylized religious compositions known as icons. Icons are paintings of significant Christian subjects and events, which are created in a canonically defined style. Through their innate qualities of composition, subject matter, and color scheme, for nearly two thousand years icons have served as portals to a higher domain.

Western Christians, especially Protestants, typically respond to these images with some down-to-earth questions:

- Why are the facial expressions so fixed?
- Why do the icons appear to be two-dimensional?
- Why the colorful robes? Do the colors mean anything?

- Why did our guide insist that icons are written, not painted?
- Why are some icons covered in silver or gold?
- Why does Jesus hold his hand in the same position in so many icons?

Each of the authors of this book comes from a different Christian background. Elizabeth Zelensky is Russian Orthodox, a visiting professor at Georgetown University with an academic background in history. Lela Gilbert is a professional writer from California with Protestant roots. Before we begin to explore questions and the contrasts and commonalities between Orthodox, Protestant, and Catholic perspectives, we want our readers to be assured that we have no intention of converting anyone from one Christian confession to another. Our purpose is simply to attempt to answer questions—those listed above along with many others—in the pages that follow.

In a world increasingly torn apart by doctrinaire religious beliefs, leaving room for diversity among Christians is important. In the words of author and patristic scholar Thomas C. Oden,

A single cohesive deposit of faith, formed and shaped by the Spirit, and confirmed by free mutual consent to revelation, has persisted for two millennia. Translated into many tongues, this consensus has formed (and been affected by) many cultures without losing its core identity. The Spirit has enabled mutual general consent on key points of interpretation of canonically received holy writ in ways that are sufficient not only for eternal salvation but also for better life in this world. In this cohesive teaching lies special power to transform societies. . . . Orthodox, Catholics, and Protestants can, despite diverse liturgical and cultural memories, find unexpected common ground ecumenically by returning to classic interpreters of scripture texts that still stand as authoritative for teaching today.

An understanding of Orthodox Christianity is essential to the contemplation of icons, which continue to aid millions of contemporary Christians from Ethiopia to Russia, from Argentina to Alaska, to bridge the abyss between the material and the spiritual worlds. At the heart of this book are two questions: How is this possible? And what can icons teach non-Orthodox Christians in their quest for peace and self-understanding? Our purpose in writing is to introduce our readers to the world of spirituality expressed in icons.

More and more Western tourists are visiting lands with Eastern Orthodox religious and historic traditions. By air and land and sea, these modern pilgrims make their way to ancient churches in Greece, Turkey, Russia, and the Balkans and are awed by the magnificent architecture, frescoes, and art. Many return home with souvenir icons. After placing them on bookcases or hanging them on walls, some Christians find themselves irresistibly drawn to the icons. They also find themselves curious—and curiously ill-informed—about what these works of sacred art represent.

But Westerners need not travel far to be exposed to icons and iconography. They are displayed in religious bookstores, in art galleries, even on eBay and elsewhere on the Internet. And wherever they are encountered, the first question they raise is perhaps the most common and important one, expressed by Henry Fulton's aunt: are icons idols? By purchasing or collecting them, are we bringing idols into our homes?

The short answer is no. Orthodox believers are just as familiar with the Ten Commandments as other Christians and would not intentionally break one of them, especially in the context of worship.

Icons are an acutely sensitive reaction to the reality of Christ's incarnation. This reaction developed during centuries of struggle within early Christianity and between Christianity and Islam. As we'll see in chapter 1, a debate about icons culminated in the eighth and ninth centuries in a civil war between *iconodules* (lovers of icons) and *iconoclasts* (destroyers of icons). Just as Protestant perceptions of religious images as idols stems from sixteenth-century Europe and the Protestant Reformation, so the central position of icons in Orthodox tradition was established following these controversies in the Byzantine Empire.

From the earliest centuries of Christianity, devout iconographers have depicted the faces of biblical characters and have meticulously recorded the stories of their lives. Since the days of the early church, paintings and mosaics of patriarchs and prophets, martyrs and missionaries, the twelve apostles, Mary, the mother of Jesus, and of course Jesus Christ himself have been focal points for worship in churches and shrines, in monasteries and palaces, and even in the humblest of homes.

In Western churches, and particularly among nonliturgical denominations, these images are often looked upon as a form of art used to illustrate text, text being Westerners' primary and preferred source of spiritual insight and information. Sometimes such religious images are overlooked or rejected, either because of their unfamiliar and stylized appearance or because of their use as devotional objects. However, in the Eastern Orthodox Church, icons (*ikon* is the Greek word for image) embody a tradition much deeper and richer than that of Western representational art. This tradition reflects on a central mystery of Christendom: how did the Infinite consent to being circumscribed by the limitations of matter?

Partly because of concerns about idolatry and also because of centuries-old fractures in worldwide Christianity, the language of sacred iconography has been nearly lost in the West. The complex and enlightening symbolism, bearing witness to incarnation, to Christian doctrine, to beauty, and to truth, is overlooked. This is a sad loss, since icons and frescoes once served the universal church as "Bibles without words," as a means of accessing the transcendent realm through our limited senses. Icons have long been regarded in Eastern Christianity as "windows to heaven." In the following chapters, by taking a closer look at icons' history, theology, purpose, and language, we will attempt to open these windows to Western readers.

Some readers may find the contemplation of icons to be a helpful form of Christian meditation, not requiring controversial Eastern techniques of deep breathing or the recitation of mantras. Because contemplation of icons takes place on different levels and in myriad ways, we have included in each chapter excerpts from Lela's personal journals. These journal entries are intended to serve as reference points if you choose to reflect on icons devotionally; they are set apart from the text and open and close each chapter. We encourage readers to write their own responses to the icons discussed here, as well as to church frescoes and to other iconographic images. In this way, the soul and spirit as well as the mind can be engaged in the search for understanding and illumination.

We would like to close this introductory chapter with a poem by John Betjeman that evokes the sense of peace and quiet expectation appropriate for the first steps of our journey into the realm of the icon. Here is Betjeman's description of the interior of a Greek church:

> The domed interior swallows up the day.
> Here, where to light a candle is to pray,
> The candle flame shows up the almond eyes
> Of local saints who view with no surprise
> Their martyrdoms depicted upon walls
> On which the filtered daylight faintly falls.
> The flame shows up the cracked paint—sea-green blue
> And red and gold, with grained wood showing through—
> Of much kissed ikons.

Notes

. . . *authoritative for teaching today.* Thomas C. Oden, *The Rebirth of Orthodoxy: Signs of New Life in Christianity* (San Francisco: HarperSanFrancisco, 2003), 186.

. . . *of much kissed ikons.* John Betjeman, quoted in Kallistos Ware, *The Orthodox Way* (New York: St. Vladimir's Seminary Press, 1975), 8–9.

I

Salvation in Words and Images

[Christ] is the [icon] of the invisible God,
the firstborn of all creation.

—Colossians 1:15 NRSV

Many signs of perestroika and political change marked my 1990 trip to Kiev. Still, after hearing countless stories of religious persecution in the U.S.S.R., I was both surprised and delighted to find a tiny amber cross for sale among the clutter of tourist souvenirs in the hotel lobby. It was inexpensive, so I bought it and immediately strung it onto the gold chain I wore around my neck. I promptly forgot about it.

Two days later, I was invited by a young Russian girl to visit a nearby convent. The girl wanted to practice her English on me, and I wanted to see whatever sights I could, so off we went. It was late in the day, and as we entered the convent's dimly lit chapel, I soon found myself alone among innumerable icons, surrounded by bouquets of garden flowers and blazing candles.

All at once an elderly woman approached me, a tiny Orthodox nun, clearly a resident of the convent. She was emphatically telling me something in either Russian or Ukrainian. Every few words, she pointed at the little amber cross around my neck. And she didn't look especially happy.

I shook my head. She shook hers, frowning even more deeply.

Embarrassed and wondering if I had somehow managed to cause an international incident, I scanned the sanctuary for my "interpreter." Naturally, she was nowhere to be found.

Meanwhile, the nun seemed to be repeating herself. She looked distressed. I shook my head again and shrugged. I couldn't imagine what was bothering her so much.

Finally, she took me by the arm and led me across the chapel to a triptych, about two feet high. There was Jesus on the cross, with Mary his mother standing at his right and St. John the Baptist on his left.

I looked at the icon, at the fragrant roses that had been placed so lovingly next to it, and at the candles that represent the prayers of the faithful. All at once I understood. The elderly nun—who, old as she was, had surely survived seventy years of Soviet atheism—did not want me to wear a cross around my neck without clearly recognizing its meaning. The icon was, for her, a glimpse into the reality of Christ's sacrifice for humanity's sins. The Son of God had suffered and died for her, for me, for the whole world. Did I understand what that meant?

Somewhere along the way, I had learned to say "Jesus lives" in Russian. I nodded, placed my hand over my heart, and whispered the Russian phrase: Yesus zhiv.

For the first time, a smile lit up the old woman's face. She nodded, took both my hands in hers, squeezed them, then walked away without another word, satisfied that I knew enough about the Christian gospel to wear a cross around my neck.

For tourists and travelers, for art connoisseurs and collectors of foreign artifacts, icons are intriguing, familiar sights, especially in areas of the world that played some role in the fate of the Byzantine Empire. And they aren't all in museums and churches. They can be found in antique stores, in bazaars, and in gift shops. Many are small enough to carry home in a suitcase. But icons are puzzling and mysterious. As we've seen, some people even find them a little disquieting. For the non-Orthodox Christian to understand the icon, it is useful first to explain what it is not.

- An icon is not intended to be a work of art illustrating an incident from Christ's life or a theme of Christian theology (although some people use it as such).
- An icon is not simply a material reflection of a spiritual reality.

21

- An icon is not an accessory or accoutrement to the act of worship.
- An icon is not an idol.

An icon is so much more than a souvenir or a religious oddity. When asked to describe what an icon represents, an Eastern Orthodox Christian will explain that

- an icon is an instrument through which the knowledge of God, in his mysterious human incarnation, becomes accessible to humankind.
- an icon is the physical witness to the sanctification of matter.
- an icon is a means by which both iconographer and worshiper can participate in the realm of eternity.

Some Protestants are surprised to learn that within the Orthodox religious system, icons are central to the communication of faith. Along with Scripture and the ancient liturgy, which embodies the teachings of the earliest church fathers, they serve as means through which humankind communicates with God and through which God reveals himself to humankind.

The fact that the first Sunday in Lent is dedicated to the triumph of the veneration of icons over the iconoclasts demonstrates the theological importance of this issue. The "Kontakion [hymn] of the Triumph of Orthodoxy," which is sung on this particular day, expresses the connection between the imagery and the economy of salvation in the Orthodox worldview:

Oh Mother of God,
The Indescribable Word of the Father took flesh through you,
And therefore became describable; and penetrating with
His divine Beauty the impure image of man,

He restored it to its pristine state.
We confess and proclaim salvation in word and images.

It is interesting to note that the kontakion is addressed to the Mother of God. This is because Mary, who was a created being, became the means by which the Creator entered our world. Mary's role, and the Orthodox church's repeated references to it, can be interpreted as a vindication of creation and matter. Because Christ, the second member of the Holy Trinity, took on human flesh, the material realm has been elevated to the same level of importance as the spiritual realm.

In the Orthodox tradition, the word and the image are treated as equally important in the economy of salvation. Clearly, humans gain understanding in many more ways than through text and intellect. Images speak to the soul and spirit and reveal the creative importance of humanity's life on earth. Human beings receive salvation not only through revelation based on Scripture but also through active participation in the work of God on earth. For the Orthodox, one aspect of this participation is the creation and veneration of physical depictions of the eternal. The kontakion continues:

To those who know and receive the visions
in the forms and the figures that God himself has given
and that the prophets have seen,
to those who safeguard the tradition, both written and oral,
delivered by the Apostles and the fathers
and who, for this reason, represent holy things in images and
   venerate them:
to them, eternal memory.

It is important to understand that in their original form, icons are not factory-made ornaments or mass-produced religious trinkets. The ideal is that they would be made by devoted iconographers, who practice deep spiritual discipline as they create them. But of course most of us cannot afford original icons, so we purchase duplications.

An Orthodox iconographer, having prepared by fasting and prayer, sets about "writing" an icon; in the Russian language, the verbs *to paint* or *to draw* are used only in connection with secular painting, including the painting of religious subject matter. Therefore, iconographers do not paint icons; they write them.

The iconographer does not merely record or copy images of the world, whether of her inner psychological world or the outer "real" world that surrounds her. Instead, she writes down the text of a certain aspect of the story of our salvation, using images rather than words.

This emphasis on the word *writing* underscores icons' rootedness in the central "text" of Christianity, that of the incarnation. Writing an icon allows the iconographer to participate in the incarnation's eternal mystery; he uses matter to represent figures and events from the spiritual dimension. The worshiper, in turn, by "reading" this text through the activity of prayer, also actively participates in this spiritual activity.

Veneration versus Worship

One of the reasons icons have been misunderstood by Western Christians is because it is common to see Orthodox believers kiss them, bow before them, light candles around them, and place flowers beside them in Orthodox churches. It is essential to stress that, despite first impressions, the Orthodox Christian does not worship icons; she venerates them. The church fathers of the Eastern church made a clear distinction between *proskynesis* (veneration, bowing down, showing respect) and *latreia* (worship, adoration). Veneration is due such people as kings and queens, elders, or perhaps ancestors, while worship is reserved for God alone.

Some Protestants are very careful in their handling of the Holy Bible, not allowing it to be treated like other books. They keep it in a special place, set nothing on top of it, and handle it with great reverence. This is veneration, not worship. And it's important to keep in mind the difference between the two as we consider the celebration of matter and the material world, which has been transfigured by grace. This celebration lies at the heart of Orthodoxy.

At first glance, the word *celebration*, when applied to Eastern Orthodoxy, may seem counterintuitive. And it is certainly true that monasticism, which was central to the Byzantine Orthodox culture, has left a very strong imprint on Orthodoxy to this day. More than half of the Orthodox calendar year is marked by fast days of various degrees of severity. Orthodox services are lengthy. The liturgy alone lasts around one hour and twenty minutes for an ordinary Sunday service; the sermon adds another fifteen minutes. Traditionally no seating is available for anyone except the ill and the elderly. All of these suggest a severe asceticism, or "mortification of the flesh." Appearances are deceiving, however. Central to the Orthodox worldview is an appreciation of all creation as the evidence of God's love. A vignette from the life of St. Anthony, a leading light among the desert fathers, illustrates this focus on the material world: "There came to St. Antony in the desert one of the wise men of that time and said: 'Father, how can you endure to live here, deprived as you are of all consolation from books?' Antony answered: 'My book, philosopher, is the nature of created things, and whenever I wish I can read in it the works of God.'"

The importance of material creation is at the heart of the economy of salvation in the Orthodox faith. Humankind is the center of created life being made in the image of God, and through the gift of free will, we are the means through which God acts in all creation. In the words of St. Leontius of Cyprus, "Through heaven and earth and sea, through wood and stone, through all creation visible and invisible, I offer veneration to the Creator, and Master and Maker of all things. For the creation does not worship the Maker directly and by itself, but it is through me that the heavens declare the glory of God, through me that the moon worships God, through me that the stars glorify him, through me the waters and showers of rain, the dews and all creation worship God and give him glory."

The Holy Wisdom of God

The subject of Holy Wisdom is closely connected to the creation of the material world in the Orthodox tradition. Wisdom is sometimes depicted iconographically as an allegorical figure, the personification of eternal providence, which was present from before time began and whose culminating point is the crucifixion. This imagery illustrates the belief that God's plan for salvation could be fulfilled only through the material world.

In Orthodoxy, this belief in the divine mission of created matter is expressed through the concept and image of Sophia, the Wisdom of God. This is the poetic symbol or metaphor for the providential aspect of God's activity in the created world. Wisdom depicts matter as it participates in and reflects God's divine plan or order. The primary scriptural text supporting this concept is 1 Corinthians 1:23–24: "But we preach Christ crucified: a stumbling block to Jews and foolishness to Gentiles, but to those whom God has called, both Jews and Greeks, Christ the power of God and the wisdom of God." (See also Prov. 8:22–30; 9:1–6; Isa. 9:6; 11:2.)

While Protestants sometimes refer to events that come together in a serendipitous or nearly miraculous way as providential, an Orthodox Christian would see them as a manifestation of Holy Wisdom. Essentially, these ideas mean the same thing. When God is working out his will in the world, in his wisdom he causes events to come together according to his providential purposes. Whether the believer refers to this as providence or wisdom, the hand of God is both evident and acknowledged.

Certain icons are dedicated to Divine Wisdom, and they demonstrate this idea through three sorts of depictions:

1. Images of Christ as Logos, or of the cross as the means through which Wisdom enters the world.
2. Images of Mary, the Theotokos (Mother of God), who is the house, or the material dwelling place, of Wisdom (Isaiah 7–9; Proverbs 8–9).
3. Wisdom as an allegory, usually portrayed as a winged figure of indeterminate sex and angelic appearance, having a fiery face. This is a reference to Christ as the Wonderful Counselor (Isa. 9:6); the same Scripture refers to Christ, in the Septuagint version of the Old Testament, as the "Fiery-Faced Angel of Great Counsel." The coloration of the face and the angel's golden robes refer to the dawn of creation, at which the Logos was present.

Today there remain numerous churches and shrines, dating to late antiquity and early medieval times, that are dedicated to this concept. They can be found in the areas of Europe and Asia Minor, now Catholic, Orthodox, and Muslim, that were once under the cultural influence of Byzantium from the sixth century CE to the sixteenth century. This testifies to the importance of the Divine Wisdom in the Orthodox worldview. Besides the famous Great Church of Hagia Sophia (Holy Wisdom), dedicated by Emperor Justinian in the sixth century CE in Constantinople (present-day Istanbul), Wisdom churches are also found in Greece, Macedonia, Serbia, Bulgaria, Ukraine, and Russia.

Wisdom also appears in frescoes and mosaics, such as the ones decorating the outside wall on the eastern side of the Dormition

Cathedral in Moscow's Kremlin. In the apse overlooking the altar, the interior frescoes echo the same subject. Other examples are found in the monumental mosaic of the Virgin as Unbreachable Wall in the Sophia Cathedral in Kiev. Farther west, a Sapienta Wisdom mosaic is found in Monreale, Sicily. All of these are evidence of Byzantium's widespread influence in medieval Europe.

Mary and the Saints

As we will see in the pages that follow, not only is Christ depicted in iconography but so also are Mary, his mother, and the saints. A few words must be said about the veneration of Mary as background to our understanding of iconography. All biblical Christians believe that Jesus Christ is the only-begotten Son of God, born of a virgin, and that Mary of Nazareth was that virgin. All believe that she is "blessed among women," that she serves as a primary example of complete obedience to God in her "yes" to the angel at the Annunciation, and in her humility as expressed in her song, the Magnificat (Luke 1). Her faith in Christ as redeemer placed her not only in the story of his crucifixion and resurrection but also in the Upper Room at Pentecost, when the church was empowered through the outpouring of the Holy Spirit.

The Orthodox church venerates Mary in its liturgy as "more honorable than the cherubim and beyond comparison more glorious than the seraphim," thus superior to all created beings. The perfect union of human and divine, personified by Christ, makes possible the sanctification and glorification of all human nature. The human being who personifies this glorified nature is Mary. In adoring the humanity of Christ, the Orthodox venerate his mother, from whom he received his humanity. Mary, who bore the Second Person of the Trinity in her womb, was the house in which Wisdom dwelt, clothed in flesh and blood.

28

The role of the Virgin for the Orthodox is that of intercessor between others and her son; the wedding feast at Cana of Galilee is the model for her intercessory activities. Although Jesus was present, those who were worried about the lack of wine at the wedding approached Mary. She, in turn, told Jesus about the crisis. She then instructed the others, "Do as he tells you."

The veneration of Mary, as well as other saints, is another point at which Orthodoxy and Catholicism differ profoundly from Protestantism. As with *sola Scriptura*, this facet of our common Christian faith also seems to be open to different interpretations. The saints are not mediators between God and humans; this would, of course, usurp Christ's unique function as mediator. Along with Mary, they are our intercessors and our protectors.

Protestants sometimes explain that they reject the whole idea of venerating saints, and particularly Mary, because it recalls pagan practices. Father Sergius Bulgakov, one of the most well-known Russian Orthodox theologians of the twentieth century, offers this interesting response: "The deep veneration of the Virgin in Orthodoxy sometimes shocks outside observers because it seems analogous with paganism. Such critics discover the prototype of the Virgin in Isis and other female divinities. But even if it were admitted that paganism had a certain obscure prescience, the difference between these goddesses and the Virgin, who is a glorified creature . . . is too evident to warrant any comparison."

Orthodox and Catholic believers explain that the church is the body of Christ and that it is composed of all its members, both living and dead. Those who belong to Jesus Christ (Rom. 1:6) are with Christ after they die. They are saved and have received the power and life of Christ. It is to these saints—including the Virgin Mary—that the prayers for the intercession of saints are directed. They are fellow Christians as well as witnesses of earthly trials and tribulations; they are the cloud of witnesses mentioned in Hebrews 12:1.

Like Protestantism, Orthodoxy does not believe that the role of saints is based on special merits of those saints before God. There is no *quid pro quo* in the Christian faith, and the principles of the counting house are useless in the economy of salvation. Saints are simply those who love God and their fellow man and who, for the sake of this love, undergo, through a heroic effort over mind and body, a purification of the heart. Sergius Bulgakov explains, "Sanctity has as many forms as there are human individualities. The sublime work of holiness always has an individual and creative dimension. Saints help us not by force of their deserts, but by force of the spiritual freedom in love that they have acquired through their spiritual efforts. This freedom gives them the power to represent us before God in prayer and also in effective love for human beings."

In the biblical Greek language, *holy* means "set apart." As Protestants claim, all Christians are indeed set apart for holiness through the process of sanctification. Throughout the centuries, however, there have been women and men who have lived such exemplary lives that they serve as models. They are called saints in both the Catholic and Orthodox traditions, and they provide the kind of heroes and heroines for all believing Christians that are so sadly lacking in today's world.

Beyond Space and Time

The Orthodox believe that as windows into the eternal realm, icons exist beyond time and space, thus they are not defined as belonging to one or another epoch or as expressing the national peculiarities of one or another people. However, for the purposes of this book, it may be helpful to place the history of icon veneration within the context of early Christianity.

The origin of icons is shrouded in mystery. Pictorial depictions of the central aspects of the Christian faith, either in the form of symbols such as the Good Shepherd or the Lamb of God or as more complex acronyms such as ICTHUS, the fish sign, are found in locations where early Christians were known to gather. The catacombs in Rome contain many of these images.

Eusebius, the bishop of Caesarea in Cappadocia (265–340), wrote the *History of the Church*; it is to him that we owe much of our knowledge of the first centuries of Christianity. He writes, "I have seen a great many portraits of the Savior, of Peter and of Paul, which have been preserved in our time." What makes this evidence even more valuable is the fact that Eusebius was leery of these portraits, suspecting them to be remnants of paganism and thus a danger to true Christianity.

When Constantia, sister of Emperor Constantine, visited Jerusalem, she asked Eusebius for an image of Christ. The bishop sternly rebuked the royal lady: "The form of a servant [human] as assumed by the Logos in Jesus Christ is no longer in the realm of reality." Eusebius went on to say that Constantia would do better to contemplate Christ "only in the mind."

Evidently the tendency for iconoclasm was present from the early centuries of Christianity. However, the first articulate theology of iconoclasm did not develop in written form until the eighth century. Pressures from a triumphant and militant Islam attacking the borders of the Byzantine Empire pushed the Byzantines to reexamine their commitment to the veneration of images. Emperor Constantine V Copronymos (741–775) was the first secular ruler to openly question the orthodoxy of icon veneration.

This concern about icons was inextricably linked with a christological issue that underlay the first one thousand years of Byzantine theology. Questions about the degree to which Christ was human, and therefore able to be represented or painted, galvanized Byzantine society from the fifth through the ninth centuries. The Seventh Ecumenical Council at last put an end to this controversy in 787. The attendees of the council adopted the argument of one of the most well-known of the Eastern church fathers, St. John of Damascus.

In his treatise *On the Divine Images: Three Apologies against Those Who Attack the Divine Images*, St. John writes, "In former times, God, without body or form, could in no way be represented. But today, since God has appeared in the flesh and lived among men [as Jesus Christ] I can represent what is visible in God. I do not venerate matter, but I venerate the creator of matter, who became matter for my sake, who assumed life in the flesh, and who, through matter, accomplished my salvation. Never will I cease to honor the matter which brought about my salvation."

It is upon this understanding that the Orthodox church has built its ancient belief in the veneration of icons and continues to reverence them as sources of revelation. This belief is based on the teachings of the early church fathers, whom virtually all Christian denominations respect. It is in this spirit of respect that we hope to introduce icons—their language, their message, and their beauty—to Western Christians.

In the following chapters, we will explore the many layers of meaning that enliven several historic and beloved icons and frescoes. Color, as one of the basic attributes of God's creation, is fundamental to conveying meaning in Orthodox iconography. In his book *Theology of Color*, Eugene Trubetskoy wrote in 1916,

The range of meanings is as infinite as the natural range of colors we see in the sky. First comes the blues, of which the icon painter knows a great many—the dark blue of the starry night, the bright blue of day, and a multitude of light blues, turquoise, even greenish blues after sundown. However, only the background is seen as blue; against it unfolds an infinity of the sky's other colors: the glitter of stars, the red of dawn, the red of nocturnal storms or distant fires; and also the rainbow's many hues: and finally, the gold of the midday sun. In icons we find all these colors in their symbolic, other-worldly meaning. All are used by the artist to divide the empyrean from the terrestial plane of being. This is the key to the ineffable beauty of the icon's color symbolism.

We will consider the symbolic meaning of numbers and the messages they carry. One example of this (and there are many) has to do with images of Christ's face, which is sometimes depicted with two small strands of hair on his forehead, at the hairline. These are said to represent his dual nature—human and divine. In iconography, the number three refers to the Trinity, six to humanity, twelve to the Old Testament tribes of Israel and to the New Testament apostles, and eight to the resurrection.

We will reflect on the unique qualities iconographers have assigned to various figures, making it possible to identify them, no matter in which century the icon was created. For instance, St. John the Baptist can be recognized by his long, unkempt hair and rough garments, referring to his life in the wilderness. St. Paul has a high forehead and a brown beard; St. Peter has curly gray hair and beard.

We also will see the effect of inverse perspective, which, rather than creating a three-dimensional scene, draws the viewer into the two-dimensional world of the icon. We will see, too, how icons deliberately avoid a realistic appearance. The faces on icons are often fixed in their expression because iconographers avoid the emotional dimension in order to focus on the transfigured, the resurrected, the sanctified nature of those depicted. As Dennis Bell writes in *Sacred Art Journal*, "An icon, then, has a sense of 'otherworldliness,' un-natural, not of this world. We know that in seven out of eleven post-resurrectional appearances, Christ was not immediately recognized: Mary mistook Him for the gardener; the men on the road to Emmaus didn't recognize Him until the 'breaking of the bread' (which, of course, is interpreted in a eucharistic sense). He appeared through closed doors, but was not a ghost. He remained flesh and blood, but 'deified' flesh and blood."

33

It is in these ways that an icon becomes a window into heaven. It transports the viewer into the heavenly realm and foreshadows a time when all the faithful will be transformed into glorified humanity. Just as Christ is the firstborn of all creation, in the prophetic world of the icon, those who follow him will at last become truly Christlike, transformed into his image by the renewing of their minds and spirits.

Chuck Smith Jr., an American Protestant pastor, was visiting Kostroma, a historic Russian city northeast of Moscow, where his hosts took him on a tour of the Ipatievsky Monastery. There, in the monastery's Trinity Cathedral, are a series of frescoes, painted around 1684 by a team of artists under the direction of Gury Nikitin and Sila Savin. Although these artists were involved in the decor of several other Russian churches, many believe the frescoes in the Trinity Cathedral to be their finest work, consisting as it does of eighty-four compositions extended in horizontal tiers, depicting an astonishing array of biblical stories and characters.

As he stood in one area of the cathedral, the colors and scenes that surrounded him captivated the American. He saw the miracle at Cana. The raising of Lazarus. The Last Supper in Jerusalem. He knew the stories well. He had preached about them for decades.

"But all at once," he said later, "I found myself in the book of John. And it wasn't the same as reading the book of John or studying the text. It was far more than that. I was there. I was in the midst of the story. And as I slowly moved on, I was in the book of Acts. I stood and stared, and in some

*way I don't completely understand, it seemed to be coming
to life before my eyes."*

Notes

. . . *by "reading" this text through the activity of prayer, also actively participates
in this spiritual activity.* The reader interested in pursuing the study of Orthodox
Christianity in the English language would do well to begin with Bishop Kallistos
Ware's book *The Orthodox Way* (Crestwood, NY: St. Vladimir's Seminary Press,
1999). For a more historical approach, see Alexander Schmemann's *The Historical
Road of Orthodoxy* (Crestwood, NY: St. Vladimir's Seminary Press, 1963). The
liturgical life of the Orthodox Church is explained in another wonderful book by
Schmemann, *For the Life of the World: Sacraments and Orthodoxy* (Crestwood,
NY: St. Vladimir's Seminary Press, 1967). For a specifically Byzantine focus, see
John Meyendorff's *The Byzantine Legacy in the Orthodox Church* (Crestwood,
NY: St. Vladimir's Seminary Press, 1982). The best introduction to the function
and meaning of icons in the Orthodox world remains Leonide Ouspensky and
Vladimir Lossky's *The Meaning of Icons* (Crestwood, NY: St. Vladimir's Seminary
Press, 1983). The simplest and most direct access to the heart of Orthodoxy may
be found through reading the spiritual diary of an anonymous nineteenth-century
Russian peasant, known in its English translation as *The Way of a Pilgrim*, tr.
Gleb Pokrovsky (Woodstock, VT: Skylight Paths, 2001).

. . . *read in it the works of God.* Evagrius of Pontus, quoted in Kallistos Ware,
The Orthodox Way (rev. ed., Crestwood, NY: St. Vladimir's Seminary Press,
1995), 43.

. . . *God and give him glory.* Ibid., 54.

. . . *Byzantium's widespread influence in medieval Europe.* Sergius Bulgakov's
Sophia, The Wisdom of God: An Outline of Sophiology (Herndon, VA: Lindisfarne
Books, 1993) is the clearest and most eloquent introduction for the Western reader
to the Eastern Christian concept of the created world as the reflection of Divine
Wisdom, despite its controversy in some Orthodox circles. Pavel Florensky's *The
Pillar and the Ground of the Truth*, tr. Boris Jakin (Princeton, NJ: Princeton Uni-
versity Press, 2004) reflects a more widely acceptable position on this subject. For
an interesting discussion of the pictorial depictions of Divine Wisdom, see Donald
M. Fiene's article "What Is the Appearance of the Divine Sophia" in the *Slavic
Review* 48, no.3 (fall 1989): 449–76. Eugene Rice's scholarly monograph *The
Renaissance Idea of Wisdom* (Cambridge, MA: Harvard University Press, 1958)
provides the reader with a parallel Western context for this same idea.

. . . *evident to warrant any comparison.* Father Sergius Bulgakov, quoted in
Daniel B. Clendenin, ed., *Eastern Orthodox Theology: A Contemporary Reader*
(Grand Rapids: Baker, 1995), 68.

. . . *effective love for human beings.* Ibid.

... have been preserved in our time. Eusebius, *History of the Church*, 20, col. 680.

... which brought about my salvation. John of Damascus, *On the Divine Images: Three Apologies against Those Who Attack the Divine Images*, or. 1, p. 94:1245A.

... beauty of the icon's color symbolism. Eugene Trubetskoi, *Icons: Theology in Color*, tr. G. Vokar, intro. G. M. A. Haufman (Crestwood, NY: St. Vladimir's Seminary Press, 1973).

... but deified flesh and blood. Dennis Bell, "Holy Icons: Theology in Color," *Sacred Art Journal*, 15(1): 2–12.

2

Andrei Rublev's Icon of the Holy Trinity

The LORD appeared to Abraham near the great trees of Mamre while he was sitting at the entrance to his tent in the heat of the day. Abraham looked up and saw three men standing nearby. When he saw them, he hurried from the entrance of his tent to meet them and bowed low to the ground. He said, "If I have found favor in your eyes, my lord, do not pass your servant by."

—Genesis 18:1–3

It is the color, first of all, and then the gentle movement and relaxed posture of the figures that draws me in. There is a circular motion to the composition, and beyond its

visual effect, it speaks to me of the conversation between the "angels."

The translucent colors shimmer with light, radiant in their expression. The Father is garbed in blue and wears an outer garment of luminescent gold, an indefinable shade, unearthly and mysterious. The Son, although earthly in the deep red-brown of his robe, is shawled in the blue of the heavens and marked with the royal gold of his Father's kingdom. The Holy Spirit is depicted in heavenly blue shrouded with the green of life: "The Lord, the Giver of Life."

The Son's eyes are fixed upon the Father, interceding. The Father's eyes are fixed upon the Son, listening. The Spirit awaits, fulfilling his role as both embodiment and articulation of the divine will.

Are the eyes of the Spirit focused on the chalice that contains the eucharistic meal? It could be said that the Eucharist is the Spirit's greatest earthly work, empowering the natural elements with supernatural energy, feeding the world with the Bread of Life. Perhaps as he hears the plans of the Father and the Son's assent, he perceives his role of continuing the sacrifice for all eternity. Perhaps his somewhat sorrowful posture indicates foreknowledge of the Son's broken body and shed blood, the Son whose hands are not yet scarred and seem to be blessing the cup.

The subject of Andrei Rublev's Holy Trinity icon is three angels, disguised as travelers, who are enjoying the patriarch Abraham's hospitality beneath the shade of the oak of Mamre, as described in Genesis 18:1–8. To contemplate the icon spiritually requires time spent prayerfully and reflectively in its presence—a period of solitude and, perhaps, silence. Spiritual reflection also requires familiarity with the biblical story.

To fully understand the icon is a demanding proposition. A grasp of its historical and liturgical significance must begin with a journey across centuries and continents to the waning years of the tenth century. At that time, Vladimir was grand prince of Kievan Russia.

Prince Vladimir was baptized in 988 into the Christian church, and at that time he established Byzantine-rite Christianity as the official religion of his people. Before his conversion, the prince was pagan, a follower of a polytheistic animism that blended the beliefs of his Viking ancestors with those of the indigenous Slavic population. The Slavs, living in the Dniepr River Valley and around its tributaries as far north as the Gulf of Finland, had been conquered by the Vikings almost two hundred years before.

The story of Prince Vladimir's search for a new religion has been recounted in numerous medieval chronicles and legends. Feeling the intellectual emptiness of polytheism, the prince sent out envoys to survey the major monotheistic religions. Upon their return, after an unenthusiastic review of Judaism and Islam, the envoys described the Orthodox worship at the Basilica of Hagia Sophia in Constantinople as stunning. "Then we went to Greece [sic Byzantium] and the Greeks led us to the edifices where they worship their God, and we knew not whether we were in heaven or on earth. For on earth there is no such splendor or such beauty, and we are at a loss how to describe it. We know only that God dwells there among men, and their service is fairer than the ceremonies of other nations. For we cannot forget that beauty."

Before long, the sumptuous, mysterious rituals of the Orthodox church found their way into Old Kievan Russia, and the veneration of icons was also introduced. Sacred paintings, along with the magnificent choral music and processions, could not fail to impress a people gifted with an innate artistic sensibility. As we will see, the Eastern Slavs later created their own masterpieces in this field. These were inspired by their Greek teachers but also reflected the reality of their particular society and their natural surroundings.

Two hundred years later, at the dawn of the thirteenth century, Genghis Khan's armies burst out of the steppes of Mongolia and, in a spectacular campaign of destruction and subjugation, swept before them everything from the Sea of Japan to the Carpathian Mountains. The Slavic civilization was destroyed. Kiev was burned in 1240, and Prince Vladimir's descendents fled northeast, to the relative safety of the forests around Moscow.

St. Sergius and Andrei Rublev

In the fifteenth century, the Princedom of Muscovy, medieval precursor to the modern Russia, was still burdened with an onerous and demeaning servitude, which undermined its very existence as a sovereign state. Tribute payments to the Tatar-Mongol overlords had bled the country dry, while civil strife and internecine warfare among the demoralized ruling clans all contributed to an atmosphere of unrest, insecurity, and dissension. A chronicle of this period reports, "With brother raising sword against brother, the land fell into emptiness and devastation."

Against this backdrop of civil strife and continuing military incursions by foreign troops, a monastery was founded by St. Sergius of Radonezh, one of the most charismatic of all Russian Orthodox religious figures. It was here, a quarter of a century later, around 1411, that a monk named Andrei Rublev began painting his vision of celestial peace and harmony, expressed through a vision of the Christian dogma of the eternal concord of the Father, the Son, and the Holy Spirit—the Old Testament Trinity. In many ways the story of his masterpiece is not only his story but also the story of his spiritual mentor, St. Sergius.

Rublev's elderly spiritual mentor—his "father-confessor"— was a monk who had known St. Sergius personally. And the values Rublev strove to express in the Holy Trinity icon were those of St. Sergius, whose *leitmotif* was the quest for unity through love. According to Sergius' hagiographer Epiphanius, the monastery's cathedral, for which Rublev eventually would paint the icon of the Holy Trinity, was dedicated to the "single in Essence, Life-giving and Indivisible Trinity . . . in order that through its constant contemplation we may conquer our fear of the hateful disunity of this world."

Russian saints are often overlooked in the Western church, and it is interesting to look at the life of St. Sergius, who lived from 1332–92 and has much in common with the better-known Italian saint, Francis of Assisi. Like Francis, Sergius was born the son of a nobleman who felt no inclination for the life of a warrior or a court official, the two normal pursuits for a boy of his class. He had a meek and mild disposition, a dislike of dissension and faction, and a passionate desire to contemplate God through a life of prayer and meditation. These qualities drove him away from his parents' aristocratic home into the trackless forests that covered the northern half of the medieval Russian state in an impenetrable canopy.

Sixty kilometers northeast of Moscow, with his own hands Sergius hacked a tiny hermitage out of the brush, and there he devoted himself to contemplation, prayer, and toil. He dedicated his abode to the Holy Trinity, expressing for the first time what would be the central theme of his life.

Stories are told about the saint's many encounters, similar to those of St. Francis, with animals and birds. These seem to be the first expressions of Sergius' hospitable nature. During terrible winters, packs of wolves often surrounded his hut, coming right up to his door. Again and again St. Sergius prayed; again and again the wolves quietly dispersed.

It is also said that a bear kept him company for years. St. Sergius shared his bread with the beast, dividing it evenly between them both. When, as often happened, there was only enough for one, Sergius gave the whole portion to the bear. "The bear is not gifted with reason," he explained, "and therefore knows the value of neither patience nor abstinence." When there was no food left and the beast would cry, the saint would speak to it encouragingly and lovingly, explaining that soon God's providence would provide.

One day a flock of beautiful birds soared around the hermitage. In a vision, a voice told Sergius that these were the souls of brethren who would inhabit his religious community in future years.

As word of the hermit's piety spread throughout Muscovy, a number of monks searched him out, joining him in his forest habitat. Eventually, despite his reluctance, Sergius' little community grew, and he became the abbot of the Monastery of the Holy Trinity. As human nature would have it, the more monks joined the community, the more difficulties arose. Intrigues and ambitions poisoned the atmosphere, and finally St. Sergius could tolerate it no longer. One day he was gone, leaving everyone behind. Eventually his contrite brethren recalled him. He returned, as focused as ever on the importance of self-denial as a requirement for unity.

St. Sergius' monastery came to be known far and wide for its hospitality. In St. Sergius' view, this emanated from a host's total immersion in the needs of his guests. Under St. Sergius' leadership, Holy Trinity Monastery became a ready refuge for travelers on their way to the northeast frontier of the Muscovite state—the lands of the upper Volga and the Urals. No one was turned away, neither rich nor poor, noble nor peasant. The monastery was a haven of social harmony in a state rife with class conflicts. No one's needs were left unfulfilled, including those of children. To this day, toys made by St. Sergius himself for boys and girls traveling with their parents are among the most precious of relics kept in the monastery.

The first steps toward laying the foundation for a politically sovereign and unified Russian state were also linked with Holy Trinity Monastery. It was St. Sergius who blessed Prince Dimitry Donskoi before the Battle of Kulikovo, the first Russian victory against the Tatar-Mongol overlords in 1380. He sent two of his monks, Peresvet and Osliaba, to accompany the prince into battle. Its victorious conclusion assured the eventual independence of Muscovy from Tatar overlordship and, finally, peace.

St. Sergius' life consistently expressed the theme of unity between man and man, man and nature, and man and God. For him, true hospitality was the means by which this theme was most frequently articulated.

It was just seventeen years after St. Sergius' death that the monastery requested an icon of the Holy Trinity from Andrei Rublev, who by then was a famous iconographer. The Holy Trinity Monastery had been Rublev's home from early childhood, so the theme of the Trinity would have been a familiar subject for him. Now he was chosen to express this theme in a public form.

In every Orthodox church, the second icon to the left of the main altar gate (if you stand facing the iconostasis), called the temple icon, always depicts that event or person or manifestation of the Godhead to which that particular church is dedicated. Rublev's Holy Trinity became the temple icon of the Trinity Cathedral in the Trinity-Sergius Monastery, as it came to be known after the death of its founder.

While Rublev was doubtlessly following the inner voice of inspiration in his choice of subject, he also was giving substance to a deep-seated longing for peace and concord at all levels of society in strifetorn Muscovy. During Rublev's lifetime, fifteenth-century Muscovy remained fraught with uncertainties. The church was split by accusations of heresy. Various branches of the ruling family of Muscovy were fighting a war of succession. Meanwhile, Tatar raids, the depopulation of cities, and the Black Plague all served to make the life of the average Muscovite brutal and short. In the face of all this, a curtain was lifted by Andrei Rublev, revealing a world of boundless and immeasurable peace. It was a revelation of everything Muscovy so sadly lacked, and as such it resonated, and continues to resonate, with all people of goodwill. It was because of this yearning that his icon spoke to the Russian people so powerfully and why they responded with prayer and veneration. Rublev's contemporaries sensed the icon's uniqueness from the time it was first placed in the iconostasis of Trinity Monastery. Pilgrims from all over Muscovy and beyond streamed in to see it.

Shortly after his death, Rublev became one of the few iconographers to be officially beatified by the Russian Orthodox Church; he is called St. Andrei. None of the more commonly accepted signs of saintliness, such as miraculous cures, seem to have been associated with him. It was, instead, the extraordinary power of the Holy Trinity icon itself that provided the main evidence of Andrei Rublev's holiness. His depiction of the three angelic visitors from the realm of peace was of such beauty that there could be no quarreling about the divine source of energy that guided the artist's hand.

History of the Image

The visitation scene from Genesis depicted in the Holy Trinity icon was familiar to the people of the Middle East from ancient times. Like the stories of the Garden of Eden and the flood, it was recorded from the beginning of history. Both Jews and pagans venerated the oak of Mamre; pagan sacrifices were abolished there only in the fourth century of the Common Era, during the reign of Emperor Constantine I. And according to Julius Africanus, a depiction of Abraham and the angels was hanging on the oak when he visited the site in 314 CE. Eusebius of Caesarea, as quoted by John of Damascus in his *Third Discourse in Defense of the Holy Icons*, also mentions this composition. It appears in mosaics decorating the walls of Santa Maria Maggiore Basilica in Rome (432–440) and the Church of St. Vitalis in Ravenna (546–547).

The early Christian church interpreted Abraham's guests as a premonition of the events surrounding Christ's baptism by John, when the voice of the Father and the appearance of the Holy Spirit as a dove affirmed Jesus as the beloved Son of the Father. In fact, the angelic visitation to Abraham was considered the first biblical revelation of God's triune nature. The symbolism of the three angels emphasized the eternal nature of Christ's relationship to God the Father and the Holy Spirit.

St. Augustine of Hippo, writing at the turn of the fourth century, mentioned this image in his famous commentary on the fall of Rome to the barbarians in his *City of God*: "The Lord appeared to Abraham by the Oak of Mamre in the form of three men, who undoubtedly were angels." In referring to the men as angels (Genesis refers to them only as men), Augustine was following a tradition, perhaps established by Hebrews 13:2, which reads, "Do not forget to entertain strangers, for by so doing some people have entertained angels without knowing it."

The Old Testament depiction of hospitality, so faithfully lived out in St. Sergius' monastery centuries later, had expanded and deepened within the Christian worldview, extending far beyond the customary Middle Eastern respect for strangers. Now the idea of hospitality reached cosmic proportions, because once the Trinity was fully revealed through the incarnation of Jesus Christ, the divisive effects of the Edenic fall of man were reversed. Finally, when the Holy Spirit descended on the apostles at Pentecost, not only was humanity redeemed by the death and resurrection of Jesus Christ but all of God's earthly creation was redeemed as well.

45

Another famous icon addresses a different aspect of the change that overtook the material world once God's Spirit was poured out on creation at Pentecost. The Descent of the Holy Spirit is a composition depicting the twelve apostles as they sat around the table in the Upper Room. The Holy Spirit is about to descend on them. Beneath the table yawns an abyss, and in this abyss stands the figure of an elderly King Cosmos, who symbolizes the material world, creation after Eden. A broken chain hangs down from his hands. What does this mean?

The chains that bound unenlightened matter have at last been broken. A new age has begun, one in which man and nature have united in the harmony made possible by the Holy Spirit. Since Pentecost, all humankind has been invited into fellowship at God's table. Abraham's tent has expanded to include the whole world in its hospitable embrace.

Andrei Rublev's Old Testament Trinity is simultaneously a glimpse into the earthly and the eternal spheres. As a material artifact, it carries a vast amount of information about the specific time and place of its creation. As the depiction of the mystery of the Holy Trinity, it offers a look into the sphere of eternal verities, beyond time and space.

Such is the mysterious timeliness of each and every icon; it is of this world and yet at the same time not of this world. Today, given its familiarity, it is hard to imagine that the trinitarian vision in the form of the three angels depicted in Andrei Rublev's icon was barely known in Russia before his masterpiece. Upon reflection, however, perhaps it is not surprising that the icon, celebrating harmony and concord, was painted during an exceptionally troubled and divisive era of Russian history.

Icons are intended to respond to deep questions, and every age has its own set of problems that trouble the heart. For this reason, depictions of the canonically sanctioned subjects of iconography such as the Holy Trinity, Christ, Mary, the mother of Jesus, and the saints and angels often reflect the historical circumstances experienced by the artists who painted them. Thus, an icon may be considered an expression both of individual faith and of the manifestation of a civilization's aesthetic values and material possibilities. Troubled times have often produced icons of tranquility; times of peace and plenty often bring forth icons that stress asceticism in an attempt, perhaps, to restore balance between material and spiritual values.

The Symbolism of Rublev's Holy Trinity

Rublev's Trinity is replete with meaning. Let us first turn to its physical design and colors, then examine its textual foundations. The three angelic figures, gracefully inclining toward each other in silent and endless conversation, create a circular pattern. The pattern formed by their figures echoes the sacrificial chalice of the Eucharist, also circular, which is the visual centerpiece of the composition. Unity and harmony, peace without end—the true state of the Triune God—is thus depicted. Of this trinitarian unity, Maximus the Confessor (600 CE) writes, "It is in this blessed and most sacred peace that unity is achieved which surpasses the mind and reason." The angels are grouped, from left to right, in the order established by the Nicene Creed:

We believe in one God . . .
We believe in one Lord, Jesus Christ . . .
We believe in the Holy Spirit . . .

Color is an integral element of the icon's language. The luminous blue, common to the garments of all three angels, symbolically points to the single substance of the Godhead. The indistinct coloration of the far-left angel's cloak is a direct reference to the ultimate impossibility of depicting the First Person of the Trinity. The second

47

angel, as the image of Christ, is depicted in the clearest and most defined manner; he is the only member of the Trinity with a basis in historical evidence and description. The spring-green cloak of the Third Person, the Holy Spirit, refers to him as the Spirit of Life and to the sanctification of nature and all creation.

As V. N. Lazarev, one of the most respected art historians of the Soviet era, noted, Rublev was an innovator in terms of color. He did not emulate the somber shades of Byzantine iconography in his Trinity. Instead, he adjusted his palette to match the colors of the Russian countryside around him. His icon echoes the white of the birch trees, the green of the budding groves in springtime, the gold of the rye fields, and the blue of the cornflower.

The angels' staffs (often referred to as "architects' measures" in Old Church Slavonic texts) and the draftsman's square depicted on the front plane of the table refer to the measuring, ordering, and architectural subtext of Christ as Logos and as Wisdom (1 Cor. 1:24; Prov. 8:22–32).

The icon's author alludes to the historical meeting of Abraham and the three angels in a minimalist fashion. The painting shows a stylized oak, Abraham's house, and a mountain. Abraham and Sarah are missing. Thus, without abolishing its historical meaning, Rublev shifts the worshiper's focus from the biblical event to the deeper and more profound realm of spiritual truth.

The angelic figures and the eucharistic chalice at the center of the composition provide the key to its theological meaning: this icon speaks of more than the Genesis visitation. Rublev's composition embodies the new relationship between Creator, man, and creation at the heart of Christian salvation. The relationship's potential was always present in the world. However, it could be manifested in history only once Christ's work had been completed and the Holy Spirit had descended upon the world.

The Holy Trinity and Pentecost

As we've seen, the theme of hospitality, which underlies the Old Testament story, is taken up, enriched, and expanded in the symbolism of Rublev's Holy Trinity. It includes not only the three mysterious travelers who stopped at Abraham's tent one hot afternoon millennia ago but also the entire cosmos. Pentecost Sunday is dedicated to the Trinity because the Holy Spirit's manifestation in the Upper Room (Acts 2) completed the full revelation of the Holy Trinity's presence in the world. We will examine its liturgical meaning in a moment. Its symbolic nuances undoubtedly influenced the way the Orthodox believer perceived Rublev's icon; when the Holy Spirit descended on the apostles, founding the historical church, the earth was also touched by the Spirit, becoming once again a hospitable home to humankind. Nature turned from foe to an unfathomable, life-giving wellspring of joy and wonder.

An Orthodox Pentecost hymn illustrates the feeling of awe at divine providence and the resulting unity of all creation:

> Blessed is our Lord Jesus Christ,
> since he sent us most wise fishers of men,
> having inspired them with the Holy Spirit,
> and thus having captured the whole cosmos
> in the net of your salvation.

This idea is further expressed in the symbolic Russian custom of decorating homes and churches with flowers and green branches on Pentecost, strewing cut grasses on the floors of the churches, and reflecting joy in nature as a manifestation of God's providence. As a result of Christ's redemption and the Holy Spirit's visitation at Pentecost, the universe has become one vast church or temple, reflecting the beauty of the Lord, bringing for all humankind the universal message of salvation.

The new covenant depicted by Andrei Rublev in his Holy Trinity icon stresses love and friendship, the bonds of host and guest. The man Abraham is the host, and the indefinable, indivisible Triune Godhead is his guest. This complements and perfects the old covenant of the Sinai commandments. In the words of an Orthodox canticle,

> The blessed Abraham saw the Trinity
> as far as men can
> and regaled It as a good friend.

Orthodox Liturgy and the Holy Trinity

Orthodox iconography and liturgy link the appearance of God in history in the form of three angels with its culmination, the fellowship of the New Testament church. For the Orthodox, the liturgy serves as both symbol and guarantee of a divinely ordered universe. It is a timeless manifestation of the Logos. In the words of a contemporary Greek theologian, Archimandrite Vasileos,

> The Divine Liturgy makes the whole world function in a liturgical way. It puts the whole of nature into Trinitarian action. . . .
> A liturgical icon speaks to you of something which has gone beyond the categories of yesterday and today, here and there, mine and thine. It addresses itself to human nature universally, to man's thirst for something beyond. . . . Through the icon, the everlasting and unchanging reality speaks without words; a reality which, in the clarity of silence and in tranquility, raises up from the deepest level that which unites everything in man."

The eucharistic symbolism of the chalice associates Rublev's composition with the paramount liturgical moment: the descent of the Holy Spirit on the bread and the wine and their subsequent transfiguration into the body and blood of Christ. When Andrei Rublev was painting this icon, the question of the efficacy of the Eucharist was raised by anti-trinitarians. For example, does the unworthiness of an officiating priest reflect on the efficacy of the sacrament? Rublev, following the position taken by the Holy Trinity Monastery, took a clear stand against this view. Instead, through his icon, he was affirming the centrality of the Eucharist to the economy of salvation: as a sacrament from God, it cannot be tainted by unworthy ministers.

The cycle of prayers offered up by the Orthodox at the Feast of Pentecost, which falls on the Sunday fifty days after Orthodox Easter, further reveals the liturgical meaning of the Trinity icon. Directly following the regular Sunday liturgy, three prayers composed by St. Basil the Great are read to the faithful, who hear them on bended knee, beginning with a call to worship:

> Come, O people, and bow down to the Triune Godhead,
> to the three hypostasis,
> let us bow to the Father as He is in the Son,
> and to the Holy Spirit.

Three prayers, to the Father, the Son, and the Holy Spirit, are read.

The first prayer calls on God the Father to forgive us our sins and bless us.

The second prayer is for God the Son to make us receptive to the Spirit of Holy Wisdom in asking for God's generous gifts.

And finally, the third prayer, to the Holy Spirit, describes Christ's harrowing of hell and presents the full picture of unity between the living and the dead, Creator and creation.

These prayers mirror the mystery of the Holy Trinity, so beautifully exemplified in St. Sergius of Radonezh's hospitable way of life and so eloquently expressed in the all-embracing composition of Andrei Rublev's icon. As twentieth-century British author Robert Byron writes, "The view [of Rublev's Holy Trinity] was a revelation, a work of unprecedented invention, to which nothing in art that I could think of offered a parallel . . . one which differed in its greatness more than I thought possible from the accepted canons of greatness."

Behind the Father is his house, with "many dwelling places." Psalm 84 sings, "How lovely is thy dwelling place, O Lord Sabaoth. My heart longs, even faints, for the house of the Lord." Before the dawn of earthly time, it was already in the Father's mind to prepare such a place for his children.

Behind the Son, a tree. Eden's Tree of Life or Calvary's Tree of Death? The oak of Mamre, yes, but more.

Behind the angel of the Spirit, a holy mountain, where his still small voice can be more clearly heard. Perhaps it is the secret place of the Most High; a lonely place, where each of us retreats from time to time.

Above all else, however, it is the peaceable conversation that speaks most to me, and the relaxed, unhurried quality of the three beings. When I was a child, I would awaken and hear the voices of my parents in the next room. It gave me a sense of security, knowing they were there, talking just out of sight. Much more comforting is the conversation of the Three, the voice of Holy Wisdom, speaking, perhaps from time to time, my name.

52

Notes

. . . *For we cannot forget that beauty.* Serge Zenkovsky ed., *Medieval Russia's Epics, Chronicles and Tales,* 2nd ed. (New York: E. P. Dutton, 1974), 67–68.

. . . *entertained angels without knowing it.* St. Augustine, *City of God,* bk. 16, chap. 29.

. . . *that which unites everything in man.* Archimandrite Vasileos, *Hymn of Entry* (Crestwood, NY: St. Vladimir's Seminary Press, 1984), 81.

3

The Vladimir Theotokos

"Do not be afraid, Mary, you have found favor with God. You will be with child and give birth to a son, and you are to give him the name Jesus. He will be great and will be called the Son of the Most High. The Lord God will give him the throne of his father David, and he will reign over the house of Jacob forever; his kingdom will never end."

"How will this be," Mary asked the angel, "since I am a virgin?"

The angel answered, "The Holy Spirit will come upon you, and the power of the Most High will overshadow you. So the holy one to be born will be called the Son of God. Even Elizabeth your relative is going to have a child in her old age, and she who was said to be barren is in her sixth month. For nothing is impossible with God."

"I am the Lord's servant," Mary answered. "May it be to me as you have said."

Then the angel left her.

—Luke 1:30–38

Battered and beautiful, the Theotokos of Vladimir is, to me, a portrait of ambiguity. It is so familiar, so ancient, so historic that at first glance it speaks to me only of myth and tradition. I think of Byzantium. Of Mother Russia. Of the pride and pomp and fate of nations, past and present.

I soon think of better things—the venerable Eastern Orthodox Church and the faithfulness of Orthodox Christian theology: the ornate stars, prominently placed on Mary's veil and shawl, proclaim Christ's virgin birth. The powerful neck of the Christ child breathes his life-giving Spirit into the Mother Church. I see Christ's tender embrace of humanity, beginning with his mother, Mary. I see the sorrow of humanity, looking upon "him who you have pierced," and of Mary as she foresees the sword that will most certainly pierce her heart.

The gold of the Christ child's robe bespeaks his divinity, while Mary's somber, earth-hued clothing recalls the weeds of mourning. She supports the child's weight, but her left hand seems hardly to touch him, as if she is about to present him to all the world.

Maybe she says, "Look at Jesus! Has any child ever been so perfect?"

Maybe she whispers the words that St. John the Baptist later proclaims: "Behold the Lamb of God who takes away the sin of the world!"

Or maybe she is silent, simply preparing herself to hand her Son over, struggling to release him to do his work.

Jesus' eyes are fixed upon his mother, but her gaze looks beyond the viewer, perhaps transfixed by some inner vision. Although her Son's embrace is wholehearted, her response is more ambiguous. She seems torn; he does not.

Beyond all the history and doctrine, as a mother reflecting on the icon, I feel again the tender touch of my own son's soft cheek pressed against mine, and of the delicate balance between holding him too closely and losing my grip on him altogether. I revisit my own early days of motherhood, and Mary's face reminds me that I might have better cherished my child's embraces if I had been less worried about so many things. What does the future hold? What if he gets hurt or falls ill? What if I am unable to love him as I should? As life would have it, those warm days of infancy passed far too quickly, while the worries remain.

My thoughts soon move from my own baby to Christ, whose warm embrace never falters, even now. I have to ask myself, Am I really able to feel it? Can I ever learn to celebrate his love and attention and constancy and to let the sadness go?

For a moment, in my imagination Mary becomes Martha, and Jesus says, "You are worried and upset about many things, but only one thing is needed." I am reminded that I will be most blessed by the presence of God if I focus my attention fully on him. As the prophet said of him centuries ago, "You will keep in perfect peace him whose mind is steadfast, because he trusts in you."

Look into the eyes of the Vladimir Theotokos. They are infinitely sad. Mary knows what will happen to this infant who strains to embrace her, cheek to cheek. She knows what the future holds; the prophetic word of old Simeon has surely said, "A sword will pierce your own soul too" (Luke 2:35).

On Holy Thursday and Good Friday, three poignant lines are read in the Orthodox liturgy as part of the Mother of God's lament, which she utters at the foot of the cross.

> Where are you going, my child,
> To where do you rush so swiftly?
> Is there another wedding feast at Cana?

How profoundly deep is the human tragedy underlying Christ's passion! All love entails suffering, but most of all maternal love, which is fraught with potentially heartbreaking situations. How can a mother guard her beloved child from the wounds that life will inevitably inflict on him? How can a mother love her child enough to let her go? A mother's boundless empathy leaves her vulnerable and open to pain and loss. Surely it is this archetypal situation that makes the mother and child imagery of the Theotokos (Mother of God) icons so compelling.

Fully informed consent and free will underlie Mary's agreement to become the mother of Jesus, the Messiah. In the words of Nicholas Cabasilas, a Byzantine theologian of the fourteenth century, "The Incarnation was not only the work of the Father, of his Virtue and of his Spirit, but also the work of the will and faith of the Virgin. God took Mary for his Mother only after having instructed her and convinced her; he was thus able to take flesh from her because she freely chose to give it to him. In the same way that God wanted to become incarnate, he wanted his Mother to bear him freely, of her own free will."

The freely chosen nature of Mary's vocation is what keeps her role from turning into destiny, or predestination. And this brings us to one of the fundamental differences between Orthodox and Roman Catholic views of Mary, the mother of Christ. The doctrine of the immaculate conception was codified as dogma by Pope Pius IX in 1854, giving official status to a belief traditionally held among pre-Reformation Western Christians that Mary was uniquely chosen from the moment of her soul's creation by God to be untainted by original sin; thus she was said to be immaculately conceived. This view of Mary evolved out of the Augustinian notion of inherited guilt. If all mortals are burdened with a corrupt will as part of their inheritance from Adam, Mary must have been immune from this corruption due to some essential difference in her makeup; she must have been immaculately conceived.

St. Augustine, however, exercised practically no influence in the Byzantine world. There the significance of the sin of Adam and its consequences were understood in quite a different way. The inheritance of the fall, according to Orthodox theology, was mortality rather than sin. The wrong choice made by Adam brought in passion, corruption, and death, which St. Paul called the "wages of sin," but not inherited guilt. In the Orthodox understanding, sin and the guilt that derives from sin can only be the result of a freely chosen act. Conversely, if an act occurs as an automatic consequence of humankind's nature, it cannot be deemed a sin.

The rebellion of Adam and Eve against God was their personal sin, according to Orthodoxy, and not part of a larger pattern of inherited guilt. Ambiguities in translation intensify this essentially different understanding of human nature. The Latin translation of Romans 5:12, which was the key text in St. Augustine's understanding of original sin, can be rendered in English with these words: "As sin came into the world through one man, and through sin, death, so death spread to all men, for in Adam all men have sinned."

The original Greek version of this verse, however, reads, "As sin came into the world through one man, and through sin, death, so death spread to all men because all men have sinned." In other words, according to the Greeks, when humans sin they become like Adam, but not simply by being the descendents of Adam do they inevitably sin. The inheritance from Adam is mortality, not guilt. And since no one doubts Mary was mortal, there is no need for the doctrine of the immaculate conception in Orthodox theology. Mary achieves salvation not despite her flesh but because of her flesh, through her freely given agreement to participate in God's plan to save the world: "Behold the handmaid of the Lord; be it unto me according to thy word" (Luke 1:38 KJV).

The fact that the Theotokos is pure, by her own will and goodness rather than by some predestined fate, raises her high above any hint of erotic chivalry as depicted in Western medieval European art and literature. This point is illustrated by the hymn sung during the Christmas Eve vespers:

What shall we offer, O Christ . . .
The heavens offer you angels,
The earth brings you its gifts,
But we men offer you a Virgin Mother.

Unlike Eastern Orthodoxy and Roman Catholicism, the Protestant understanding of Mary's nature is that she was neither born without sin nor sinless throughout her life. She is not venerated, and her identification as "Mother of God" is, unless understood in the context of the early church's concerns with Christ's dual nature, not used. Images of Virgin and Child, although often seen at Christmas, are otherwise rarely displayed in Protestant churches.

Protestants, except in faith communities that express belief in the intercessory role of the communion of saints, do not offer prayers seeking Mary's assistance or intercession. In efforts to stand against what has been called "Mariolatry" in the Roman Catholic tradition, some Protestants have rejected the powerful example set by Mary's incomparable faith and obedience to God's call, not only in the mysterious conception of God's only begotten Son but in the subsequent years during which "the Son of Man had no place to lay his head," during the growing foreboding about his doom, and finally, during his abuse, torture, and ignominious death on the cross.

In dramatic contrast, prayers to the Theotokos occupy a large place in Orthodox liturgical life. Of the twelve major feast days in the Orthodox church calendar, five are dedicated to the Virgin: the Virgin's Birth, the Virgin's Presentation at the Temple, the Annunciation, the Dormition of the Virgin, and the Protection of the Veil. Besides these feast days, innumerable prayers are addressed to her. Her name is constantly invoked during services, along with that of her Son.

According to ancient writings, St. Luke the Evangelist painted three icons of the Theotokos from life. These icons should be understood as part of apostolic tradition in the same sense as when we speak of the apostolic liturgy, or apostolic rules. These articles of belief go back to the apostles not because the apostles themselves wrote them but because they bear the apostles' authority and character. According to tradition, the Virgin gazed upon the icons painted by St. Luke and exclaimed, "May the grace of him whom I bore and of myself be forever with these holy icons."

Visions of the Theotokos

And this brings us back to the Vladimir Theotokos, which was based on one of the three types of icons credited to St. Luke. In the Russian church they are the Smolensk-Hodigitria, the Virgin of the Sign, and the Protection of the Veil, or Intercession.

The Vladimir Theotokos, which represents the Hodigitria type of icon, was painted in Byzantium—probably in Constantinople—at the end of the eleventh century. It has spent, however, most of its thousand years of existence in Russia. It is currently housed in the Tretiakov National Art Gallery in Moscow. A few words about images of the Theotokos in Byzantium and medieval Russia will help place this particular icon in its historical context.

The Vladimir Theotokos is an excellent example of painting from the golden age of Byzantium, whose art is characterized by "dignity and graciousness, restraint and balance, an undisturbed refinement and . . . harmony with religious emotion," according to Byzantologist A. A. Vasiliev. This particular icon is the product of the last full-fledged flowering of a civilization that was precariously balanced on its pinnacle of artistic and political power. By the end of the eleventh century, the fortunes of the Byzantines were on the wane. The devastating defeat of the Byzantine army by the Seljuk Turks in 1076 at Manzikert, compounded by the rape of Constantinople in 1204 by Western crusaders, fatally weakened the empire. Its final fall in 1453 to the forces of the Ottoman Sultan Muhammed II was something of an anticlimax, long expected by all.

The particular compositional type upon which the Vladimir Theotokos icon is based is known as the icon of Lovingkindness (in Russian *Umileniie*), a translation of the Greek *Eleousa*, which carries connotations of mercy, compassion, pity, and tenderness. In the words of St. Isaac of Syria, these emotions flow "when a man's heart burns for all creation—men, birds, demons, and all creatures. At their memory and sight his eyes shed tears. . . . This is why he prays hourly, for dumb creation, for the enemies of truth, for those who harm him, [that] they should be preserved and shown mercy; he prays also for the reptiles with a great compassion which wells up in his heart without measure until he becomes likened in this to God."

The Vladimir Theotokos is the physical image of motherhood transformed into compassion for all creation. In her we see a woman transfigured and magnified into her full spiritual potential. And this, of course, is the task of all true icons: to reveal human beings in their full eschatological meaning through contact with divine grace.

Queen of Heaven

This aspect of the Vladimir Theotokos, however, should not blind us to the other reality of the Byzantine image of the Mother of God, in which Mary reigns as Queen of Heaven. Hymns to the Theotokos, which can be traced back to the earliest years of the Christian church, are replete with monarchic imagery. Mary is addressed as Sovereign Lady (*Vladichitsa*) time and again. Her full-length figure is invariably pictured wearing scarlet slippers, a type of footwear Byzantine law reserved for members of the imperial family.

Dean Miller, a Byzantine historian, has even made the argument that the Byzantine emperor, as a ritual and theological concept, was symbolically a bigendered figure combining imagery taken from the figure of Christ and from the Theotokos. The true emperor operated in a symbolic universe that was bifurcated; he was both master of the masculine sphere of justice and war, and also high ruler in the sphere of mercy, nurture, and even miracle, qualities connected to the feminine principle.

Similarly, Emperor Justinian referred to Constantinople's great church, Hagia Sophia, as "the mother of our kingdom." The Virgin's body as the carrier of divine order in the form of the Holy Child thus logically could become a metaphor for sacred space. This metaphor could be expanded to include a city, any city, as a possible celestial Jerusalem.

The Virgin Oranta (praying with arms raised up at shoulder level and carrying no child) mosaic that dominates the apse in the Saint Sophia Cathedral in Kiev is a wonderful illustration of this aspect of the Theotokos. The inscription over the arch of the central apse that encircles the Oranta is taken from Psalm 46:5: "God is in the midst of her, she shall not be moved. God will help her, early, early." The juxtaposition of Psalm 46 with the mosaic of the Oranta, in which "she" refers to Jerusalem, underscores the role of the Theotokos as protector of Christian cities, such as Kiev or Constantinople, as reflections of celestial Jerusalem, the city of God.

Leading the Armies to Victory

A Byzantine hymn whose first line addresses the Virgin as "victorious leader of hosts" introduces yet another aspect of the Theotokos figure in Byzantine culture, that of palladium or victory bearer. Both Byzantine and Slavic armies in the Middle Ages carried banners bearing the image of the Theotokos as a sign of divine protection for their cause. The cult of various Theotokos icons as city palladia—among them the Vladimir Theotokos—was well established all over medieval Russia. The Smolensk Virgin, for example, was the patroness of the city of Smolensk. The Vladimir Theotokos icon came to be linked with the city of Moscow. A brief excursion along the icon's historical path helps us understand what it meant to the ancestors of contemporary Russians.

According to the ancient Kievan chronicles, the icon was brought to Kiev from Constantinople in the twelfth century. In 1155 it was sent to the northeast frontier of the Kievan federation, to the land of Suzdal. This event indicates the seismic shift in power and influence from Kiev, the old capital of the eastern Slav federation, to the northeast frontier, around the present capital of the Russian Federation: Moscow.

Holy Trinity, Andrei Rublev

The Vladimir Theotokos

Transfiguration of Christ, Theophanes

Dormition
of the
Virgin

The Sinai Pantocrator

Iconostasis, Russian Orthodox Cathedral of
St. John the Baptist, Washington, D.C.

While Kiev was destroyed by the Tatar-Mongol invasions of the thirteenth century, the *coup de grace* being its immolation in 1240, the city had been gradually losing its importance for at least a century. The capture of Jerusalem by the Western crusaders in 1099 opened up a direct trade route between Western Europe and the Orient. The Viking-founded state of Kievan Rus', whose main reason for existence was the commercial trade route to Constantinople, consequently lost its importance.

In 1161, as a further token of a new order looming on the horizon, the icon was taken by Prince Andrei Bogolubskii to the frontier town of Vladimir. Here he began to rule in an unprecedented way. Stressing his descent from Byzantine autocrats, he consulted with neither his elder courtiers nor the townspeople. Although his innovations proved rather unpopular (he was assassinated during a palace coup in 1175), his style of governance eventually became the signature style for his indirect descendents: the grand princes and, finally, the tsars of Muscovy.

Three official church holidays are dedicated to the Vladimir Theotokos: May 21, June 23, and August 26. All three celebrate victories over Tatar and Turkic invasions that threatened the city of Moscow between 1395 and 1521. These were pivotal years for the establishment and consolidation of the Tsardom of Muscovy.

The August 26 date commemorates the circumstances under which the Vladimir Theotokos actually left Vladimir and was taken to Moscow for good. In 1395, Tamerlane, the great Central Asiatic conqueror, was nearing the city of Moscow with his invincible hordes. The Grand Prince of Muscovy, Vasilii I, sent for the Vladimir Theotokos as the last hope for the Muscovites. The icon's journey lasted ten days; the roads by which it made its way to the capital city were lined with people on their knees praying, "Oh Mother of God, save the Russian land!" The grand duke, his family, and his court met the icon several miles before the city gates and accompanied it on foot, with a full church procession to the Dormition Cathedral in the Kremlin.

It is said that that very night Tamerlane had a dream in which a woman clothed in the sun appeared to him, accompanied by an army of winged angels carrying golden spears. The next day, Tamerlane's wise men interpreted the dream to mean that the divine intercessor for the Russians before the throne of God, the mother of the Christian God, had appeared to the Asian military leader. Tamerlane immediately gave the order to sound the retreat, since he could not hope to be victorious over the Queen of Heaven. Moscow was saved.

The icon remained in the Dormition Cathedral in Moscow until the revolution of 1917, at which time it was placed in the Tretiakov Art Gallery. Until then, all coronations took place in the Dormition Cathedral, under the watchful gaze of the Vladimir Theotokos. Other pivotal moments in both the spiritual and the political lives of Moscow were marked by the presence of the Vladimir Mother of God.

The death in 1598 of Tsar Fedor Ioannovich brought the eight-hundred-year-old Riurikide dynasty to a close. Boris Godunov, Tsar Fedor's brother-in-law, was elected to the throne by the semblance of a popular assembly, along with a great deal of behind the scenes intrigue. In order to underscore his legitimacy as contender to the throne, the procession of petitioners that made its way from the Kremlin to the convent where Boris was staying with his sister, the widowed Tsarina Irene, was led by the Vladimir Theotokos.

During Napoleon's invasion of Russia, in 1812, the Vladimir Theotokos, along with the Smolensk Virgin, were carried out to the troops in order to strengthen their morale. This took place on the eve of the Battle of Borodino, which proved crucial in the eventual defeat of Napoleon. Once again tens of thousands of soldiers knelt alongside the road when the icons passed on their way to a

church service in the field attended by Emperor Aleksandr I and
Field Marshall Kutuzov, the Russian commander-in-chief.

Help from a Compassionate Intercessor

The role of palladium, however important it has been in its civic
aspect, does not exhaust the spiritual and symbolic meaning of
the Mother of God's image for the Orthodox. It bears repeating
that for most of the world's Christians, the Virgin Mary's ultimate
function is that of intercessor for the human race before the throne
of the Almighty. She is one of us, of the same substance as the
rest of humanity. Yet the all-powerful love felt for her by her Son,
Jesus Christ, puts Mary into an absolutely privileged position as
an intercessor. She has become, in the eyes of both Catholic and
Orthodox believers, a living bridge between heaven and earth. The
"Akathistos Hymn" in its second chant describes this intercessory
capacity in the following way:

Hail, oh hidden Sense of the Ineffable Plan. . . .
Hail, oh Forecast of the marvels of Christ!
Hail, oh Fountainhead of truths concerning Him.
Hail, Celestial ladder, by whom God came down!
Hail, oh bridge leading earthly ones to heaven.

For the Protestant believer, it may be helpful to think about the
intercession of Mary in light of living partners in prayer. Many of
us have a friend or loved one who prays for us, someone we can
count on to intercede for us when troubles arise or decisions must
be made. Perhaps it is a parent, a relative, a spouse, or a friend. If
that person were to die, would we stop asking her or him to pray
for us? If we reflect upon the communion of saints, the "cloud of
witnesses" made up of believers who have passed on from this

life to the next, we might well be encouraged to continue to ask our Christian loved ones to intercede on our behalf.

It would be in a similar sense that we might ask for the Virgin Mary's intercession. Just as Jesus requested from the cross that John take his mother home, so we can invite her to be a part of our earthly families and to pray with and for us about the issues that concern us. Mothers, particularly, may find great comfort in inviting her to intercede. Who could better empathize with us as we care for our children, with our joys and sorrows, our hopes and fears?

A Russian apocryphal story vividly illustrates the compassion of the Virgin; in this text she asks the Archangel Michael to allow her a glimpse of the sinners suffering in hell. This he proceeds to do in Dante-like detail. The Virgin is horrified and begins to cry in empathy with the sufferers. She then goes to heaven and asks all of the saints and angels to beg God to have mercy on the sinners. She says if they will not, she herself will go back to hell to suffer with the sinners!

She raises her hands in prayer to her Son and says, "Have mercy, Lord, upon the sinners, for I have seen them and I could not endure. Let me be tormented together with the Christians. . . . Have mercy, Oh Lord, upon the sinners, the creation of thine own hands . . . who in all places say, 'Holy Lady, Mother of God, intercede for us.'"

Eventually the Lord relents and declares that he will suspend all torments in hell from Maundy Thursday to Holy Pentecost (fifty-three days), saying it would be so "by the mercy of my Father who sent me to you, and through the intercession of my Mother who has wept much for you, and through Michael the Archangel and through the multitude of martyrs who have labored much in your behalf."

This apocrypha, which was repeated in the form of a well-known pilgrim song for nearly a thousand years until the Russian revolution, is a wonderful example of the perception of the Theotokos in the Orthodox system of values. She is the ever-sympathetic, ever-caring mother to whom anyone can turn, no matter what. She is seen as the last resort of all creation, being the first of all creatures.

Leonid Ouspensky, philosopher and art historian, has written about the Lovingkindness Theotokos, exemplified by the Vladimir Mother of God. He explains that she is the most striking example of the fact that every human feeling expressed in an icon acquires its full meaning through its contact with divine grace. The empathy of motherhood—the most instinctive part of human nature—becomes transfigured into compassion for all creation. Contact with the Son of God transforms mother-love into all-embracing tenderness and grief for the whole world, for everything and everyone in it. In the "Akathistos Hymn," Mary is

> The shelter of the world,
> Wider than the clouds.

Even though Mary's sorrowful face nearly eclipses the radiance and affection of her Son, tenderness is the theme of the icon. Distracted and distraught, she loves him so much that she cannot quite receive his love in return.

God help me! As I welcome Jesus Christ as the only begotten Son of God, help me turn my eyes toward his face. Make me able to fully delight in his embrace. Only in receiving the fullness of his love can I find strength to bear the pain that life inevitably entails. Bring to my mind "whatever is true, whatever is noble, whatever is right, whatever is pure, whatever is lovely, whatever is admirable." If anything is excellent or praiseworthy, teach me, dear God, to fix my mind on these things as manifestations of your Son's incarnation and of his Holy Spirit's continuing presence in the world.

Notes

. . . he wanted his Mother to bear him freely, of her own free will. Nicholas of Cabasilas as quoted in Paul Evdokimou's *The Art of the Icon: A Theology of Beauty*, tr. Fr. S. Bigham (Redondo Beach, CA: Oakwood Publications, 1996), 260.

. . . forever with these holy icons. May 21, Festal Menaion.

. . . according to Byzantologist A. A. Vasiliev. A. A. Vasiliev, *History of the Byzantine Empire*, vol. 1, 2nd ed. (Madison: University of Wisconsin Press, 1971).

. . . much in your behalf. Serge Zenkovsky, ed., *Medieval Russia's Epics, Chronicles and Tales*, 2nd ed. (New York: E. P. Dutton, 1974), 159.

4

Theophanes' Transfiguration of Christ

[Jesus] took Peter, John and James with him and went up onto a mountain to pray. As he was praying, the appearance of his face changed, and his clothes became as bright as a flash of lightning. Two men, Moses and Elijah, appeared in glorious splendor, talking with Jesus. They spoke about his departure, which he was about to bring to fulfillment at Jerusalem. Peter and his companions were very sleepy, but when they became fully awake, they saw his glory and the two men standing with him. As the men were leaving Jesus, Peter said to him, "Master, it is good for us to be here. Let us put up three shelters—one for you, one for Moses and one for Elijah." (He did not know what he was saying.) While he was speaking, a cloud appeared and enveloped them, and they were afraid as they entered the cloud. A voice came from the cloud, saying, "This is my Son, whom I have chosen; listen to him." When the voice had spoken, they found that Jesus was alone. The disciples kept this to themselves, and told no one at that time what they had seen.

—Luke 9:28–36

At first glance, Theophanes the Greek's icon of the Transfiguration of Jesus looks like a modern stained-glass window, so angular is the star, so radiant the blue surrounding Jesus. But a closer look reveals it is reminiscent of Rublev's Holy Trinity—the iridescent color of Moses' and Elijah's robes, the unusual formation of the mountains.

In the upper corners are small figures of saints softly bathed in gold. Perhaps they indicate that life in the heavenly realm is continuing, even in the midst of such an extraordinary scene on earth. These two images are repeated, a little larger, in what appears to be the depths of the earth, where the saints seem to be offering instruction. Despite the miracle, the kingdom of God must still be taught to those who will listen.

The three disciples, who are forever honored for having accompanied Christ to the mountain, are rendered helpless, unable to fully witness the event unfolding before them. Their eyes are flooded with unbearable light. Their hearts are overwhelmed with an exhausting combination of sensory bombardment, fear, and awe. And in their ears thunders the voice of all voices, affirming the incarnation: "This is my beloved Son, in whom I am well pleased. Listen to him!"

James covers his eyes; John looks almost ill. Characteristically, Peter valiantly tries to fix his eyes on the Master, his mind awhirl with wonderful thoughts. Unfortunately, he misses the point, at least for awhile.

72

The Light of the World is, for a few moments, transfigured by the light of heaven. In Philippians we read of Jesus, the Son of God,

> *Who, being in very nature God,*
> *did not consider equality with God something to be*
> *grasped,*
> *but made himself nothing,*
> *taking the very nature of a servant,*
> *being made in human likeness.*
> *And being found in appearance as a man,*
> *he humbled himself.*

—2:6–8

Here, however, the Son's humble, human likeness is briefly changed back to his heavenly glory. His role as a servant is momentarily suspended, and he is glimpsed undisguised.

His three friends were unprepared for such a sight. I imagine that because the light was holy light, their souls' imperfections must have been both evident and appalling. It is not difficult to imagine them crying out, "Lord Jesus Christ, Son of God, have mercy on me, a sinner."

For centuries, that very prayer has helped prepare hearts for the light of heaven, the light of Mount Tabor, the light of Christ's pure radiance, which persistently shines here and there in what sometimes seems to be a darkening world. Even today it can serve as a purifying flame, burning off the dross of daily life, turning our eyes, like Peter's, toward the almost-unbearable beauty of Christ.

73

The story of the transfiguration of Jesus is, for most Protestants, a fascinating glimpse into the future, when those who are in Christ will be "changed in the twinkling of an eye" into a glorified state at his second coming. According to St. Paul's writing to the church at Corinth, "The trumpet will sound, the dead will be raised imperishable, and we will be changed. For the perishable must clothe itself with the imperishable, and the mortal with immortality. When the perishable has been clothed with the imperishable, and the mortal with immortality, then the saying that is written will come true: 'Death has been swallowed up in victory'" (1 Cor. 15:52–54).

The transfiguration of Christ is not the subject of popular discussion or interest among Protestants, who tend to focus more on such issues as the crucifixion and the end times. The reason for this, perhaps, is because people are naturally more interested in matters they perceive to be relevant to them right now. Like Roman Catholics, Protestants find great personal importance in the crucifixion because it is central to their own salvation. The end times are interesting both because of their implied connection to current world affairs and their implicit promise of a better day to come. Many Protestants, however, think of the transfiguration as something that happened in the past and don't perceive it as an event particularly germane to today's world.

Orthodox Christians, however, have long embraced the transfiguration in a more meaningful and reverent way. Nicephorus Callixtus writes that St. Helena, the mother of Emperor Constantine, had a church built in honor of the transfiguration of Christ on Mount Tabor in 326 CE. There are shrines built in honor of the transfiguration all over the Orthodox world, and numerous icons of this subject exist.

74

For the Orthodox, Christ's transfiguration has deeper mystical significance, applicable to the here and now, available to all who are being transformed into his image. Theophanes the Greek's Transfiguration icon is one of many iconic expressions that communicate this story from the synoptic Gospels. Among all of the icons discussed in this book, this one may be the most intellectually challenging work, both in terms of artistic composition and religious content.

The biblical basis for the icon is found in Mark 9:2–10, Matthew 17:1–8, and Luke 9:28–36. According to the New Testament, Christ ascended Mount Tabor in the company of his disciples Peter, James, and John. Because the description of the transfigured Christ in raiment "white as light" with a face that "shone as the sun" follows Christ's statement that "some of them that stand here, which shall not taste of death, till they have seen the kingdom of God come with power" (Mark 9:1 KJV Luke 9:27), this event is eschatologically significant. Christ reveals himself on Mount Tabor as he will appear at the last judgment, shedding his earthly form as a servant, revealing his cloaked divinity. In the holiday hymn honoring the transfiguration, the Orthodox sing:

Thou wast transfigured on the mountain, O Christ our God,
Showing to Thy disciples Thy glory as each one could endure;
Shine forth Thou on us, sinners all, Thy light ever-unending.

The Gospels provide different perspectives on the story of Jesus as he and his three friends ascended the mountain. According to the version in Mark and Matthew, the three apostles fell down in awe and wonder after hearing the voice of the Father and seeing the bright cloud surrounding the Son. According to Luke, they fell asleep and awoke to see the glory of Christ. In all three accounts, Moses and Elijah appear on either side of the transfigured Christ.

The fact that Christ appeared in his divine nature, which he holds in common with the Father and the Holy Spirit, links the transfiguration to the Trinity. On the Orthodox calendar, the Feast of the Transfiguration relates to the feast days of Epiphany and Pentecost. All three extol the goodness of creation, and all three testify to the fact that Christ's incarnation tore down the wall that once separated the natural world from God's grace. The Feast of the Transfiguration celebrates the dynamic relationship between God and his creation, and the possibility of communion between these two realities, different in essence but bridged through the grace of Jesus Christ and the work of the Holy Spirit.

Two Views of Man's Earthly Potential

In Russia, Belarus, and Ukraine, down to the present day, the Feast of the Transfiguration (August 19) is known as *Iablochnyii Spas* (the Apple Savior). Traditionally, the apple harvest was left untouched until Transfiguration Day, when the first apples were picked from the tree and taken to church to be blessed. In this way, popular culture reflected the Christian belief that a chasm between Creator and creation split open when Eve and Adam ate the fruit of the Tree of Knowledge, and that that chasm has now been bridged by a new reality. In this new reality, because of Christ's completed work, the heavenly light that transfigured everything on Mount Tabor now shines once again upon all of creation, including apples.

In Ukraine, the first ears of grain are also blessed on this day. They are then taken home and tucked behind the family icons; it is with seed taken from these ears that the autumn sowing will begin.

The theological meaning of such practices revolves around three premises:

1. All relationships based on love, including that between man and God, are of a voluntary nature.
2. We have the opportunity to experience God through means other than intellectual or sensory.
3. It is possibile for our physical bodies to achieve celestial glory right here on earth, prior to the second coming.

A Great Debate

In the fourteenth century, the Orthodox church was convulsed by controversy concerning these three principles. Four church councils were called, in 1341, 1347, 1351, and 1368, in an attempt to clarify the relevant issues. The result of these councils was, in the words of John Meyendorff, "the definitive expression of the doctrine of man's deification."

The high point of these questionings occurred from 1337 to 1340. It involved a debate between Barlaam, who was an adherent of Western scholasticism and a Greek scholar from southern Italy, and Gregory of Palamas, bishop of Thessaloniki, leader of the hesychast movement. These two scholars debated the nature of the light on Mount Tabor.

Barlaam used the controversy surrounding the nature of the Taboric light to attack Gregory of Palamas and the hesychasts. Hesychasm is an Eastern Christian ascetic practice that can be traced back to the fourth century. The term literally means "a state of sobriety or impassibility." Its central tenet is that humans can, if they so choose, participate in direct communication with God, thus achieving what is called deification or *theosis*.

Gregory of Palamas, in a letter describing the proceedings of the church council that condemned Barlaam as a heretic in 1341, gives the following summary of his opponent's views: "[Barlaam says that] the light that shone on the apostles on Mount Tabor and the sanctification and grace similar to it are either a created mirage, visible through the medium of the air, or else a figment of the imagination, lower than thought and harmful to every rational soul in so far as it derives from sensory imagination."

Gregory of Palamas countered Barlaam's argument with the claim that the light on Mount Tabor was uncreated and that the apostles' ability to see it testified to the human potential for direct communication with the divine.

The Humblest of Prayers

Hesychasm, represented by Gregory of Palamas at that long-ago council, is a form of communication with God that requires a rigorous and difficult effort of will. The path is marked by a high degree of asceticism, by certain breathing exercises, and by introspection, which ultimately result in a state wherein "the intellect controls the heart, and the heart controls the intellect." Hesychasm is sometimes compared to forms of Roman Catholic monasticism and mysticism and to certain Protestant spiritual disciplines. It remains, however, unique in its practices. And despite its historical definition as a movement, it is, in fact, intensely personal.

Probably the most well-known of hesychast practices is the Jesus Prayer, which has been popularized through the English translation of a nineteenth-century anonymous Russian tract, *The Way of the Pilgrim*. The Jesus Prayer consists of the simple words "Lord Jesus Christ, Son of God, have mercy on me, a sinner." The believer repeats these words mentally through all of the waking hours until they meld into one with his or her heartbeat.

This practice appears in the novel *Franny and Zooey*, by J. D. Salinger. Salinger uses the contrast between *The Way of the Pilgrim* and Franny's superficial and empty socialite life as the central dynamic of his narrative. What Gregory Palamas defined in the fourteenth century, and what J. D. Salinger hinted at in the mid-twentieth century, seems to have been a sort of Christian humanism, in which the centrality of a Christian's place in the universe is tied to the possibility of internalizing Christ as an immanent presence in the Christian's heart.

This internalization of Christ and the ensuing deification of man or woman was explained in the fourth century, when Athanasius of Alexandria declared that the purpose of Christ's incarnation was the ultimate deification of humankind: "God became man so that man could become God." This interpretation of Christian anthropology was impossible to reconcile with the human passivity implied in Barlaam's interpretation of the transfiguration. On the other hand, there were problems with this view. The Eastern church fathers could not simply ignore the problem of how a created humanity, totally dependent on physical senses for knowledge of the material world, could actively come to know, much less become like, the uncreated, invisible, and indescribable God.

Choosing to Be Made in the Image of Christ

All of this raises a question: what exactly was it that the apostles saw, with their physical eyes, on Mount Tabor?

To answer this question without resorting to allegory, we have to focus on what Christ in his divinity had in common with the three men on Mount Tabor. The four shared the willingness to freely limit the self in the name of love. For the sake of love, Jesus surrendered himself to the will of his Father; for the sake of love, John, James, and Peter surrendered their wills to Jesus and followed him.

This willingness, which may also be termed *grace* or *divine energy*, is the ultimate manifestation of God in this world. As such, it must be freely chosen. Maximus the Confessor writes, "Since man was created according to the image of the blessed and supra-essential deity, and since, on the other hand, the divine nature is free, it is obvious that man is free by nature, being the image of the deity." Free will, at the service of the Creator, is what Christ and the apostles had in common on Mount Tabor.

It is only in this realm of will, not in the realm of nature, that any true communion between humankind and Creator may take place. In his argument, Gregory of Palamas utilized an Orthodox presupposition, the distinction between God's essence and God's energy.

Here is a summary of Gregory's basic argument:

- God in his triune and eternal essence is indeed perfect and unknowable and changeless; he is outside of time and space.
- However, through a voluntary and self-circumscribing act of love, God chose to take on a human body and suffer the consequences thereof.
- God entered the world of time and space.
- God's presence in this world is made manifest by its consequences: grace or divine energy.
- We humans can never know God's essence, since this is totally "other."
- We can, however, come to know and even participate in and communicate with God's manifestations in this world—his divine energies.

These energies emanate from the Holy Trinity. Although they were present in the Old Testament, they became more fully accessible to humankind after Christ's incarnation, through Christ. It is through these energies that we may know God in this world, and it is as the pledge of this possibility that Christ appeared to the apostles on Mount Tabor: the light which his disciples saw was the uncreated light of divine energy. "He is transfigured, therefore," writes John of Damascus in his commentary on the transfiguration, "not by receiving something which he is not, but

80

by revealing to his intimate disciples what he really is, opening their eyes and enabling them to see out of their blindness." These words were used by Gregory of Palamas in his argument that, because Christ has been transfigured, humanity, too, can be and must be transfigured through him.

This transfiguration is accomplished through a process of deification, sometimes called *theosis*, a term that is used in both Roman Catholic and Orthodox theology. It can be compared to the Protestant belief in the sanctification of believers. In the simplest terms, theosis or sanctification is the process by which a Christian is transformed into the image of God; this takes place through the power of the Holy Spirit and willing participation in spiritual disciplines. The communication between God and man transpires through the Christian's voluntary obedience to the Word of God, and through cooperation with and surrender to the Holy Spirit's guidance. As Christoforos Stavropoulos writes, "The apostle Peter describes with total clarity the purpose of life: we are to become partakers of divine nature (2 Peter 1:4). This is the purpose of life: that we be participants, sharers in the nature of God and in the life of Christ, communicants of divine grace and energy."

Orthodox theologians sometimes cite Psalm 82:6, in which God says to men, "You are 'gods'; you are all sons of the Most High," as evidence that the deified human will become a "god." Daniel Clendenin, a Protestant who writes extensively about Orthodoxy, reassures readers that this premise is not as dangerous, nor as reminiscent of Eden's temptation, as some may say: "Protestants should be reassured by the fact that Orthodoxy is careful to ex-plicitly reject any hints of pantheism in its doctrine of theosis. The general idea, that believers are transformed through mystical union into the divine nature, finds support in the Pauline teaching that the image of God, distorted but not lost in the fall, is being progressively renewed in us (Col. 3:10), so that we are increasingly conformed to the likeness of Christ (Rom. 8:29). In Paul's words, we become more like Christ and God. In Peter's vocabulary, we come to share the divine nature."

Theophanes' Icon of the Transfiguration

> Falling to the ground on the holy mountain,
> the greatest of the apostles prostrated themselves upon seeing
> the Lord reveal the dawn brightness,
> and now we prostrate ourselves before the Holy face, which
> shines forth brighter than the sun. . . .
> Having illuminated the human image which has grown dark, O
> Creator,
> Thou didst reveal it on Mount Tabor to Peter and the Sons of
> Thunder: and now bless and sanctify us,
> O Lord who lovest mankind, by the brightness of Thy most pure
> image.

Now that we've considered the Transfiguration icon's biblical background, let's take a close look at this masterpiece. What exactly is being depicted? What do the geometric shapes represent? How does the somewhat modern-looking, even abstract appearance of the image reveal its theological meaning?

Painted in Muscovy by Theophanes the Greek (Andrei Rublev's teacher) in the second half of the fourteenth century, the Transfiguration is a masterpiece of visual design and theological subtlety. Christ appears standing on the very top of a steep mountain in a six-pointed star, surrounded by a gloriole of blue in the shape of a circle. The triangular shapes of the star's rays and the circular gloriole convey a transcendental moment. For the Greeks, from the classical pre-Christian era onward, geometric forms represented the eternal and perfect world beyond earthly reality.

On either side of Christ, Elijah and Moses bow before him in attitudes of supplication. Christ is motionless in transcendent peace, and Moses and Elijah are bathed in this peace as well. The three form a perfect circle, reminiscent of Rublev's Holy Trinity.

The three rays emanating from behind Christ's body point to the startled apostles below. There is a marked contrast between the calm of the upper half and the excited dynamism in the lower half. The apostles have been exposed to an unfathomable revelation. They are bowled over by the sight of the uncreated light or energy streaming from the figure of Christ.

The impact throws them to the ground, yet each apostle's reaction is different. Words of the feast day hymn come to mind: Christ has revealed himself to each "according to his capacity." The apostles' varied reactions reveal each one's personal psychology. Peter is on Jesus' right, with his hand raised to protect himself from the almost unbearable light. John is in the middle, and James is on Christ's left side. Both James and John fall away from the light.

By Peter's position at Jesus' right hand, and by his facing the light, Peter's senior status among the apostles is confirmed. And it is he who will propose, according to the Gospel accounts, that they should all remain on Mount Tabor indefinitely, "putting up tents" for Moses and Elijah and awaiting the end of time.

John's central position underscores his emotional links with Christ, as the beloved apostle to whom Christ, on the cross, will entrust his mother.

The actual painting technique of this icon is also quite interesting, revealing the purpose of icons as pieces of transfigured matter in the Orthodox religious system. The problem the iconographer had to solve in writing the text of the Transfiguration with paints and gold leaf was how to convey transcendental reality in a world bound by three dimensions. This is where the technique of inverse perspective becomes particularly useful.

When an iconographer deliberately inverts the features of natural linear perspective, he reverses the apparent diminution of parallel lines as they recede toward a vanishing point on a horizon. In doing so, he deliberately creates a sense of disorientation in the viewer. The perspective of the icon is therefore reversed, and the viewer becomes the vanishing point for the figures depicted in the icon, not vice versa. The icon is the subject; the viewer is the object. This represents a new world, opening up dimensions beyond our familiar three. The icon's inverted lines extend out toward an infinity that we cannot fathom. In this way, the iconographer attempts to break free of the human spatial experience and to release us into the realm of infinity.

If we look closely at Theophanes' Transfiguration, or at Rublev's Holy Trinity, we are struck by the unusual ordering of the icon's planes. According to the logic of three dimensional space, objects that are farther away from the viewer should appear smaller than those closer to him. Instead, they are actually painted the same size as or larger than the figures or objects that are closer.

Yet not all objects in the Transfiguration are portrayed in inverse perspective. Most of the features in any icon are rendered in natural perspective. It is only the most important images whose perspectives are reversed, and naturally the viewer's attention is drawn to precisely these images. For example, Christ is larger than the apostles, even though he is on top of Mount Tabor, and Peter, James, and John are closest to the viewer. Similarly, in Rublev's Holy Trinity, the table around which the three angelic visitors sit appears to become larger the farther it is from the viewer, in a reverse trapezoid. Disorientation and contradiction drive home the point that human understanding based on reason and sensory data is limited. True knowledge takes this fact into account.

A further difficulty for iconographers is how to depict the nature of uncreated light. It cannot come from any external source—no sun, no moon, no candle. Lines, drawn with liquid gold known as *assiste*, convey the physical sense of light. But the attitudes of the figures—the cowering, admiring apostles—do more than any particular coloration to convey the impact of the unearthly, uncreated light. It is this living and direct appreciation of the light of divine energy and its all-powerful effect on this world that most likely prompted Paul Evdokimov to say that the iconographer painting the Transfiguration was painting not so much with colors as with the Taboric light itself.

According to Epiphanius the Wise, the iconographer Theophanes "understood the faraway and the spiritual with his mind, for he perceived the spiritual beauty through his enlightened bodily eyes." The Transfiguration, as Theophanes' greatest work, was written as an anticipation of Christ's glorious second coming. Not only does it open a perspective into eternity within the world of time and space but it also offers visual evidence of the possibility of humankind's deification here on earth. It is a brief glimpse of the mystical eighth day of creation, when all created matter will share in the eternal glory of the Lord.

Kingdoms—Earthly and Heavenly

By the fifteenth century, the passions raised by the debate concerning the nature of the light that illumined Mount Tabor ran high. In the decades before the Turkish conquest of Constantinople in 1453, members of the Byzantine church hierarchy attempted to find a doctrinal compromise with the Western church. They did so not only to preserve Christian unity but also for a more earthbound purpose: they hoped to secure Western military aid against the encroaching Ottomans.

A popular sentiment countered that attempt: "Better the Muslim yoke than Western apostasy." This view was often expressed among the ranks of the Orthodox, and one of the main points that defined the "apostasy" was the West's unwillingness to accept the uncreated nature of the light on Mount Tabor. The Council of Florence-Ferrara, which took place from 1438 to 1439, was the Eastern church's final desperate attempt, a theological compromise intended to procure military assistance from the West for Byzantium. It failed miserably. Most of the Orthodox delegates repudiated their agreement to the unifying document once they reached the relative safety of their native lands, and those who did not found their congregations very unreceptive. For instance, upon his return home, the delegate from Moscow was cast into prison for apostasy.

The council's failure to reach agreement underscored the evergrowing chasm between Byzantium and the West. This is ironic considering the fact that the influence of Greek scholars, churchmen, and emigrants fleeing the unstable conditions of the failing Byzantine Empire is central to understanding the shift in Western thinking that we have come to label the Renaissance. Indeed, the Western Renaissance foregrounding of humankind in the workings of the universe, popularly known as humanism, may be understood as St. Athanasius' Orthodox principle of deification stripped of its christological framework.

Meanwhile, from the thirteenth century in the Orthodox world proper, hesychasm, with its introspection and its focus on the individual in his or her relationship to God, became a major intellectual force in church life. In Russia, St. Sergius of Radonezh practiced hesychasm, as did numerous medieval iconographers, including Andrei Rublev and Theophanes the Greek. Hesychasm remains a powerful influence among Orthodox believers even today.

The revival of intellectual interest in hesychasm in nineteenth century Russia, led by thinkers such as the layman Fyodor Dostoyevsky, centered on the monastery of Optina Pustin, whose elders were all followers of the hesychast tradition. The leader of the Serbian autocephalous church, St. Sava (d. 1237), learned hesychast practices on the sacred mountain of Orthodox monasticism, Mount Athos in Greece, and brought it back to his homeland. Hesychasm became a strong intellectual movement in Bulgaria as well.

As we've seen, hesychasts believes it is possible for humans to embrace the kingdom of heaven while still inhabiting the kingdom of earth. The implications of this idea are revealed by one of the most popular epic poems in the Serbian language, *The Battle of Kosovo*. This poem explains the historical defeat of the Serbs at the Battle of Kosovo Pole (the Field of Blackbirds) in 1389.

In 1389, the medieval Serbs, led by Tsar Lazar, made their last stand against the Ottomans. They lost, and six hundred years of Ottoman rule followed. It is hard for us in the West to perceive this incident as a glorious victory, yet that is exactly how it has been perceived by the Serbs for centuries. Why? The answer becomes clearer when we consider the predominant role of hesychasm in Serbian intellectual and religious life during the fourteenth century. Compared with the glory of God revealed on Mount Tabor, what are the kingdoms of this earth but a handful of dust?

> There flies a gray bird, a falcon,
> From Jerusalem the holy.
> In his beak he bears a swallow.
> That is no falcon, no gray bird,
> But it is Saint Elijah.
> He carries no swallow,
> But a book from the Mother of God.
> He comes to Tsar Lazar at Kosovo,
> He lays the book on the Tsar's knee and asks . . .
> What kind of kingdom will you have?
> Do you want a heavenly kingdom?
> Do you want an earthly kingdom?
> The Tsar chose a heavenly kingdom,
> And not an earthly kingdom.
> He built a church on Kosovo,
> Then he gave his soldiers the Eucharist.

Then the Turks overwhelmed Lazar,
And his army was destroyed with him—
Seven and seventy thousand soldiers. . . .
All was holy, all was honorable,
And the goodness of God was fulfilled.

The Legend of Tsar Lazar was kept alive as an oral tradition in Serbian folk memory for centuries and continues to be studied all over the Balkans. It is a timeless anthem, extolling the reverse perspective with which hesychasm defines the kingdom of God. The message of the legend recalls St. Paul's words: "But God chose the foolish things of the world to shame the wise; God chose the weak things of the world to shame the strong. . . . The man without the Spirit does not accept the things that come from the Spirit of God, for they are foolishness to him, and he cannot understand them, because they are spiritually discerned" (1 Cor. 1:27; 2:14).

"Lord Jesus Christ, Son of God, have mercy on me, a sinner."

Like the verse of a song memorized in childhood, the Jesus Prayer has come to be a part of my spiritual life, used like a spiritual remedy for an assortment of ills—fear, danger, uncertainty, stage fright, always there to lift me when trouble threatens.

It is a prayer that came to me in middle age, not childhood. And not only to me. I am told of a Russian Orthodox man, nearing fifty, who rode his Harley-Davidson motorcycle into a disastrous accident. As he flew into the air, he anticipated the awful impact with earth. As he lay in agony, broken by the fall, he began to murmur the Jesus Prayer. Again and again he said it. The darkness lifted; light dawned. The pain diminished. Once help came, he was already on the road to recovery. He recently danced at his son's wedding.

A Protestant friend of mine, facing a terrifying health crisis, was required to have an MRI. The claustrophobic environment of the noisy machine, along with the rising threat to her future, nearly overwhelmed her. I sat at her side, holding her hand and silently praying the Jesus Prayer. She made it through the imaging series frightened but without incident or major disease. She told me afterward that she also had been praying the Jesus Prayer during the procedure.

Another friend, a Roman Catholic priest, uses the Jesus Prayer as part of his daily meditation, allowing it to quiet his mind and permeate his spirit with the peace of God.

The Jesus Prayer lies at the heart of Orthodox hesychast mysticism, but its humble entreaty, so simple and so complete, is the beginning of Christian submission to God and the end of all wrestling for control over circumstances. Old as it is, the uncomplicated plea meets the modern world head-on with its immortal appeal.

"Lord Jesus Christ, Son of God, have mercy on me, a sinner."

"Lord Jesus Christ, Son of God, have mercy on me, a sinner."

"Lord Jesus Christ, Son of God, have mercy on me, a sinner."

Notes

. . . on Mount Tabor in 326 CE. Leonid Ouspensky and Vladimir Lossky, *The Meaning of Icons,* tr. G. E. H. Palmer and E. Kadlouhsky (Crestwood, NY: St. Vladimir's Seminary Press, 1983), 211.

. . . derives from sensory imagination. Leonid Ouspensky, *Theology of the Icon,* vol. 2 (Crestwood, NY: St. Vladimir's Seminary Press, 1992), 238.

. . . the heart controls the intellect. Ibid., 235.

. . . it is, in fact, intensely personal. John Meyendorff's *Gregory Palamas and Orthodox Spirituality* (Crestwood, NY: St. Vladimir's Seminary Press, 1974) and *Byzantine Hesychasm: Historical, Theological and Social Problems* (London: Variorum Reprints, 1974) are excellent introductions to the subject of hesychasm.

. . . being the image of the deity. John Meyendorff, *Byzantine Theology* (New York: Fordham University Press, 1974), 223.

. . . divine grace and energy. Daniel B. Clendenin, ed., *Eastern Orthodox Theology: A Contemporary Reader* (Grand Rapids: Baker, 1995), 184.

. . . come to share the divine nature. Ibid., 158.

. . . by the brightness of Thy most pure image. Leonid Ouspensky, *Theology of the Icon,* vol. 1, tr. Anthony Gythiel and Elizabeth Meyendorff (Crestwood, NY: St. Vladimir's Seminary Press, 1992), 162.

. . . with the Taboric light itself. Paul Evdokimov, *The Art of the Icon: A Theology of Beauty,* tr. Steven Bigham (Redondo Beach, CA: Oakwood, 1996), 299.

. . . through his enlightened bodily eyes. Ouspensky, *Theology of the Icon,* 261.

. . . And the goodness of God was fulfilled. "The Battle of Kosovo: Serbian Epic Poems," Balkania.net. See http://members.tripod.com/Balkania/resources/history/battle_of_kosovo.html.

5

The Dormition
of the Virgin

Where, O death, is your victory?
Where, O death, is your sting?

—1 Corinthians 15:55

*Not many days ago, I learned that my ninety-year-old aunt
had died. It was not unexpected. She had been lingering in
the twilight of life for months, and her husband of sixty-
nine years—my father's brother—had been at her side day
and night, barely allowing himself to eat or sleep. For a
ninety-two-year-old, this was a level of stress and exhaustion
that might well have cost him his life too. Loved as she was,
we all knew that her time was at hand. And because she*

was an exceptionally faithful believer, by our lights her future was secure in Christ. But of course there was sadness in the news.

One morning as I reflected on her death, my eyes lifted to the wall of my living room to a reproduction of the Dormition of the Virgin icon, part of a Serbian fresco. The delicate blues and greens, alight with shimmers of gold, soothed me. I paused, trying to grasp its message, an unusual message for one with a Protestant background.

Jesus' mother lies dead, surrounded by churchmen and the apostles. Their faces are sorrowful; in fact, several of the onlookers, including St. Peter and St. Paul, seem overwhelmed with grief. Even the angels who gather watchfully in the background, their torches lit against the darkness of death, look grim. Jesus' face, too, is sad, although he holds in his arms the soul of his mother. Mary has been reborn into the heavenly realm, yet those who loved her on earth mourn her passing.

How human this ancient story, juxtaposed as it is against eternal hope. Mortality and its accompanying sorrow are inevitable. Although we know that our loved ones who are in Christ share with us the hope of eternity, we still are deeply saddened, even horrified, by the presence of death.

Although moved at times to tears when I think about my aunt, I find great comfort in this old icon. In the words of St. Paul, the ambiguity of our present journey from earth's kingdom—we are aliens and strangers here—to our heavenly home renders us known, yet regarded as unknown; dying, and yet we live on; beaten, and yet not killed; sorrowful, yet always rejoicing.

92

As we saw in chapter 3, for the Orthodox, the image of the Theotokos is the iconographic key to a "theology in color," which we have contemplated throughout this book. The Virgin Mary's image is indispensable to iconography because, as proclaimed by the Council of Chalcedon, she is the one purely human element in the incarnation. The passing away and the glorification of the Mother of God is the final affirmation of her humanity. It is also the pledge of a blessed end for all mortals.

The Dormition of the Virgin is depicted in many icons and frescoes throughout the Orthodox world. The particular image of the Dormition we are reflecting on is Serbian, part of the cycle of frescoes that grace the walls of the Holy Trinity Church in the Sopocani Monastery. Love permeates this icon. The tender love of Christ for his mother is beautifully manifested; the Savior holds a tiny swaddled babe in his arms as he stands over the death bier of his mother. The baby represents the soul of Mary, pure as a newborn child returning to the arms of her Father-Son. The image of lovingkindness and tenderness between Mary and Jesus, which we first saw expressed in the Vladimir Theotokos, is reiterated here and magnified. Christ cradles the soul of his mother, newly shorn of its fleshly envelope, in his loving arms. The circle is closed.

The Virgin's fate silently affirms that deification—the transformation of a human being into the image of God—is possible. This affirmation of hope explains the tremendous popularity of the feast day of the Dormition of the Theotokos among the Orthodox. In Russia, more churches are dedicated to this event than to any other subject. The most important church in the Moscow Kremlin, the symbolic heart of medieval Muscovy, was the Dormition Cathedral. It was the coronation site for every Russian ruler through Nicholas II, the last Romanov tsar.

93

An Apochryphal Story of Love

The feast day of the Dormition of the Theotokos, celebrated in the Orthodox church calendar on August 15 (August 28 in the Gregorian calendar), seems to date back to the fourth century. The words of the liturgical hymns sung on this day provide us with highlights of the celebration's theological meaning, a meaning that is echoed in icons of the Dormition. The verses of these hymns express awe and wonder that

> the source of Life Itself is lying in her coffin,
> this coffin may be the ladder to heaven itself.

In the feast's hymns we hear, retold, the apocryphal circumstances surrounding the death of Mary. The apostles, who were already preaching the gospel message in the four corners of the world, were miraculously enveloped in a cloudlike wind and rushed back to the Virgin's deathbed. Then the Savior himself appeared, surrounded by choirs of angels, to receive the soul of his mother. This last circumstance is a sign: this death is not death at all but her entry into life everlasting. The Orthodox sing,

> You have gone to life, since you are the mother of Life
> and your prayers will deliver our souls from death as well. . . .
> The angels, having witnessed the Dormition,
> wonder at the Virgin who is ascending from earth to heaven. . . .
> The laws of nature have been conquered in you, oh pure Virgin;
> you who having given birth retained your virginity,
> and who was able to join life with death, to remain alive after
> dying.

The tradition of Mary's body being taken up into heaven—known in the West as the Feast of the Assumption—is treated in Orthodox theology as an eschatological sign, an anticipation of the general resurrection of all believers described in 1 Corinthians 15. The very term *dormition* hints at the new relationship with death that humankind has been granted through Christ's incarnation. These were demonstrated by the Mother of God's death and rebirth into life everlasting. John Chrysostom, one of the greatest of the Eastern church fathers, elucidates this point: "It is true that we still die as before, but we do not remain in death: and this is not to die. The power and the very reality of death are just this, that a dead man has no possibility of returning to life. But if after death he is to be quickened and, moreover, to be given a better life, then this is no longer death but a falling asleep."

In the words of Orthodox theologian John Meyendorff, "The boundless expressions of Marian piety and devotion in the Byzantine liturgy are nothing other than an illustration of the doctrine of hypostatic union in Christ of divinity and humanity. In a sense they represent a legitimate and organic way of placing a somewhat abstract concept of fifth- and sixth-century Christology on the level of the simple faithful." Surely, through the image Dormition of the Virgin, this subtle doctrine of deification and its consequence, the life everlasting for men and women who love and believe, became apparent to the simplest, most untutored eyes.

One other metaphorical meaning that radiates from the Dormition theme has to do with Sophia, the Holy Wisdom of God. The Orthodox cathedrals dedicated to Holy Wisdom in Novgorod and in Kiev, two of the oldest churches in the territory of the former Soviet Union, both have Marian feasts as their parish feast days. The temple icon of the Dormition Cathedral, in the Sergius-Trinity Cathedral Monastery, is the allegorical figure of Wisdom as the Fiery Faced Angel. Mary's mission is thus emphasized through the Wisdom theme. For the Orthodox, Mary is the house wherein dwelt Wisdom (the Logos or Christ as the Word); she is also the symbol of the church, mother of all believers. And so the apostles gather at her deathbed, just as they once gathered with her in the

Upper Room when the Holy Spirit descended to enliven the newly founded church (Acts 2).

Father Sergius Bulgakov writes,

> The church believes that, dying a natural death, [Mary] was not subject to corruption, but, raised up by her Son, she lives in her glorified body at the right hand of Christ in the heavens. In her is realized the idea of Divine Wisdom in the creation of the world, and Divine Wisdom in the created world. It is in her that Divine Wisdom is justified, and thus the veneration of the Virgin blends with that of the Holy Wisdom. In the Virgin there are united Holy Wisdom and the Wisdom of the created world, the Holy Spirit and the human hypostasis. Her body is completely spiritual and transfigured. She is the justification, the end, and the meaning of creation. She is in this sense the glory of the world. In her, God is already all in all.

Born in Balkan History

Sopocani Monastery, where the Dormition of the Virgin icon is located, lies in the region of Raska, near the center of the medieval Serbian state. Its extraordinary frescoes were completed between 1263 and 1270, and the unknown iconographer who painted them was undoubtedly a man of genius. To quote noted art historian Desanka Milosevic, "The work of the master of Sopocani is superior to all other paintings of medieval Serbia, because it is the product of a superb talent and of the noblest artistic aspirations. In the paintings of Sopocani, all the faces seem to radiate benevolence and calm. The beautiful figures, full of exalted energy, seem to harken to some inner silence and harmony."

Subtle light permeates and shines from this composition even today, although its gold background has almost completely vanished due to the damage caused by centuries of exposure to the elements. The Turks burned and demolished Sopocani Monastery in 1689 and carried off the lead from the church roof. The monks did not return after this, and it remained empty and deserted for more than two hundred years. The fact that a significant number of the frescos remained intact enough for restoration to be possible in the 1920s speaks volumes about the high quality of the original work.

The placement of the dormition scene on the western wall of the church, traditionally the location of depictions of the last judgment, underscores the subject's eschatological meaning. The dormition must be seen as a premonition of or precursor to the general resurrection, which will take place before the last judgment.

The apostles are arranged in rhythmic groups; they face the spectator, but their bodies are slightly turned toward the bier. All of them radiate strength, beauty, and genuine sorrow, which seem to well up from deep within them. The technique of the iconographer was to paint the faces, hands, and feet in warm colors laid on thickly, so that the impression of almost physical materiality could be created. Meanwhile, the clothing is light, nearly transparent.

Angels with staffs and torches in their hands cluster around the Virgin. In classical art, the staff was the mark of a messenger. We also see the influence of the Roman Empire, whose ruins were scattered throughout the landscape of medieval Serbia, once the empire's Balkan hinterland. The architectural details in the background of the composition, with its precise rendering of porticoes supported by marble columns with Corinthian capitals, all acknowledge the subtle presence of classical antiquity, as do the classically draped robes of the apostles.

The angels' faces suggest a subtle combination of tenderness and austerity. Their beauty is not of this world; a greenish wash marks them as belonging to a different order of beings than the human apostles. The whole composition is permeated with various shades of blue. This is the traditional color of the Virgin; during

Marian feasts, the clergy wear azure vestments and the church is decorated with sapphire-blue hangings.

While angels in Russian versions of the Dormition of the Virgin are usually represented by one token pair, here whole choirs of angels fill the background of the composition. Just as choirs of angels accompanied Christ's entrance into this world, so they cluster about his mother as she leaves it. Just as the infant Jesus was wrapped in swaddling clothes, so is the newborn soul of Mary.

The curtain hanging on the portico, on the left-hand side of the composition, is the traditional iconographic reference to the curtain veiling the inner sanctuary—the Holy of Holies—of the temple in Jerusalem. This curtain often appears in icons depicting incidents in the Virgin's life—her presentation at the temple, the annunciation, and the dormition and others—since Mary's historical life was linked so closely with the temple in Jerusalem. The curtain is also a metaphor for the Virgin herself; she became the new temple within which the Lord came to dwell.

Back to Tsar Lazar and the Field of Blackbirds

Such a beautiful expression of Christian hope needs to be understood in its historical setting. After the fall of the western half of the Roman Empire to Germanic invaders in the fifth century, its eastern half, which we now call Byzantium, was forced of necessity to go it alone. Despite their many disputes with the West, Byzantium's inhabitants continued to call themselves Rom, or Romans, until the fall of Constantinople in 1453.

One of the Byzantines' strategies was to create a network of vassal or client states along the borders of their realm. Religion played a major role in this system; from the ninth through the tenth centuries, the imperial government made a concerted effort to convert their pagan neighbors—Slavs living to the north and west—to Eastern-rite Christianity. The Cyrillic alphabet, whose characters form the basis of the written language of the Serbs, Montenegrians, Macedonians, Bulgarians, Ukrainians, Belarusians, and Russians, was devised by two Byzantine churchmen, St. Cyrill and St. Methodius. They created this alphabet to help communicate in writing to the illiterate Slavs the basic texts of Christianity. This translation took place at the beginning of the conversion effort in the second half of the ninth century.

Very soon after their conversion to Christianity, while remaining under the cultural influence of the Byzantines, both the Bulgarians and the Serbs began to strive for political independence. As was typical of the times, the adoption of religious symbolism in the interest of political independence very quickly took place. The Monastery of Sopocani, the site of the Dormition fresco, as part of this political-cultural pattern, was built by King Uros I of Serbia (1243–76). King Uros was the grandson of Stephen Nemanja, erstwhile subject of the Byzantine Empire, but also founder of the medieval Serbian ruling dynasty.

Stephen's son, Stephen Nemanja II (1196–1228), was a prudent diplomat and warrior who fulfilled his father's dream of Serbian independence. He accomplished this by taking advantage of the temporary collapse of the Byzantine Empire after the sack of Constantinople during the Fourth Crusade in 1204.

By the time of King Uros I, Serbia stretched from the present-day borders of Hungary and beyond, all the way to Greece. Uros carried on an ambitious political program, cultivating extensive ties with his neighbors to the west as a way of countervailing the ever-present danger of being reabsorbed into the greater Byzantine Empire. King Uros' wife was a French princess named Helene. His mother was Anna Dandolo of Venice, daughter of Doge Enrico Dandolo, the infamous leader of the Fourth Crusade.

These family ties are recorded in a fresco located on the southern wall of Sopocani's Holy Trinity Church. The composition, known as *The Death of Anna Dandolo*, bears a striking resemblance to the Dormition of the Virgin fresco on the western wall. Queen Anna is depicted lying dead on a bier with richly embroidered pillows and coverlets. Above her stands King Uros with his sons, Queen Helene, and noblemen, and at her head stands her daughter, who bends over her full of grief and tenderness. Above the bier is an angel who is cradling Anna's soul, represented as a swaddled infant. A monumental Last Judgment is painted directly above Queen Anna's death scene.

Thus, the royal dynasty of Serbia sought legitimization and prestige through the identification of a pivotal moment in its family life—the death of Queen Anna—with a pivotal moment in the life of the Queen of Heaven. The tombs of King Uros I, Queen Helene, Queen Anna, King Stephen, and other close relatives are all located within the Sopocani complex.

Sopocani was an important and prosperous monastery from its foundation until the end of the fourteenth century. The later history of the monastery, however, was determined by the political circumstances that affected the state as a whole. After the Battle of Kosovo in 1389, so powerfully described in the epic poem of the same name, the Serbian defeat, and the consequent penetration of the Ottoman armies into Serbia, the monastery buildings were demolished and burned down by the Turks. The monastery was rebuilt during a period known as the "despotate," when Serbians were ruled by their own leaders, who were actually appointed by and owed ultimate allegiance to the sultan.

In the sixteenth century, the monks living in Sopocani had to leave once again to avoid a Turkish onslaught. This time they took the body of King Stephen Nemanja with them. The Turks demolished and burned the monastery again in 1689. It was abandoned until the twentieth century, between the two World Wars. The bulk of the restoration and historical preservation work was done after World War II. Thanks to these efforts, today our eyes can feast on the lovely shimmering blue surface of the Dormition fresco. But once again this work of art finds itself dangerously close to yet another war zone, this time the Albanian-Serbian conflict, which continues to threaten in neighboring Kosovo.

As with Rublev's Holy Trinity, we can only wonder that such icons radiate serene and transcendental peace in the midst of the dark maelstrom of human passions and ambitions that seems to eternally swirl about them. Dostoyevsky was so right a century ago in his summary of the human condition: "Are you aware that mankind can do without the English, that it can also do without Germany, that nothing is easier for mankind to do without than the Russians, that it can live without science or even bread. Only *beauty* is absolutely indispensable, for without beauty there is nothing left in the world worth doing. Here is the entire secret; all of history right in a nutshell."

Today, as I contemplate the icon, I find myself particularly aware of the angels. They are light-bearers, on duty in a setting where they appear to be foreign, a little out of place, like a military contingent in a distant land, not sure what will happen next and faced with a scene of great sorrow. Yet how long can such sorrow continue when they accompany the one who said, "I am the resurrection and the life"?

The image is a fascinating study, silently reiterating the promise that light overcomes darkness, hope prevails over despair, and death is swallowed up in resurrection. And how comforting to know that angels exist not only in ancient stories but are with us today. Thinking about their continuing presence, surrounding the children of light, I remember a children's chorus.

101

All around march the warriors
Fierce and bright as the sun.
They were sent to protect me
Till the last battle's won.
I can hear distant singing
Praise the King who has died.
Oh, at last, come tomorrow,
May I stand by His side?

Notes

. . . on the level of the simple faithful. John Meyendorff, *ByzantineTheology* (New York: Fordham University, 1974), 165.

. . . In her, God is already all in all. Sergius Bulgakov, "The Virgin and the Saints in Orthodoxy," quoted in Daniel B. Clendenin, ed., *Eastern Orthodox Theology: A Contemporary Reader* (Grand Rapids: Baker, 1995), 67.

. . . some inner silence and harmony. Olivera Kandic and Desanka Milosevic, *Sopocani Monastery Guidebook* (Belgrade, 1986), 37.

. . . all of history right in a nutshell. Paul Eudokimov's free translation from the Russian of Dostoyevsky's *The Possessed*, vol. 3, ch. 1. While composing the novel *The Possessed*, Dostoyevsky wrote the following passage in his notebook: "The Holy Ghost is an immediate comprehension of beauty, a prophetic awareness of harmony, and so a steadfast striving for it." F. Dostoyevsky, *The Notebooks for The Possessed*, ed. and intro. E. Wasioled, tr. Victor Terras (Chicago: University of Chicago Press, 1968), 212.

6

The Sinai Pantocrator

"This is my Son, whom I love; with him I am well pleased. Listen to him!" When the disciples heard this, they fell facedown to the ground, terrified. But Jesus came and touched them. "Get up," he said. "Don't be afraid." When they looked up, they saw no one except Jesus.

—Matthew 17:5–8

The face of Christ has been depicted in countless ways. Some of them—the wan and effeminate, the raging and cruel—are unconvincing. Others, like this Sinai Pantocrator, are startling in their possibilities. Much has been made of this ancient icon's striking similarities to the image in the Shroud of Turin. Could it have been reproduced from a

portrait of Jesus painted by an admirer during his lifetime? It is certainly an image of great dignity and authority. And symbolized by the jeweled book, it is a fitting communication of "the Word made flesh."

Sometimes called the Christ of the Angry Eye, the image has long been said to bring condemnation to the hearts of those who view it while hiding sin in their hearts, and to offer blessing and peace to those who view it with a contrite and humble spirit. The face of the Savior for me, however, does not look angry so much as intriguingly asymmetrical. It is the face of a real man with a somewhat inscrutable expression, which seems to flicker and change as I study it. The dark hair plays against the golden halo, with its faintly visible outline of a cross. The face, too, has a slightly golden hue—Christ in glory but clearly a man who is approachable, even beckoning. For reasons I cannot express, it is a face that has more than once comforted me and has more than once reduced me to tears.

It is the face of a friend.

I wonder if the scene behind Christ's shoulders is Jerusalem, perhaps the New Jerusalem, from which he will rule and reign. As for his right hand, I always have to stop and remember that it is blessing me, not making a point or singling me out for a reprimand.

And finally, my eyes focus on the neck, which, like the eyes, is also asymmetrical. It reminds me, like nothing else, that this man, this incarnation of the eternal God, was formed of muscle and bone and was clothed in skin, skin that bruised, skin that burned in the desert sun, skin that ripped, skin that bled, skin that felt and touched, skin that was warm with life.

After the transfiguration, when the heavenly glory of Christ was revealed, as we've seen, his disciples were overwhelmed with awe and fear. Jesus quieted them and told them not to be afraid. They glanced around uneasily. Moses and Elijah were gone. There was no evidence of the one who had spoken in authority and exhorted them, "Listen to him." Only Jesus remained.

But by now their view of Jesus had been radically changed. By now they knew that this rabbi whom they had befriended was no ordinary man, nor was he simply a prophet. He was, as Peter had affirmed not so long before, "the Son of the Living God." After Mount Tabor, he told them pointedly that he would die and would be raised from the dead. They struggled to understand, beginning to catch glimpses of his role as both man and God. The Sinai Christ represents that mystery of Christ's human and divine nature, which lies at the heart of Christianity.

Of the icons discussed in this book, this is by far the most ancient, dating back to the sixth century. In some ways, it is also the most enigmatic. The identity of the master iconographer who painted it is unknown, and its origin is veiled in legend. Some say that no mortal hand could have painted an image so exceptional and that this icon is clearly the work of angels. Others connect it, because of numerous visual similarities, to the mysterious Shroud of Turin, the purported burial cloth of Christ, which is now housed in a church in northern Italy.

Father Justin, curator at the Monastery of St. Catherine in Sinai, Egypt, explains the process used to date the icon.

> If you have fifteen manuscripts of a particular text, exhibiting textual variants, you can compare the variants and decide which one is likely to be the earlier reading and which to be the derivative. You can then arrange them in order, in what is known as a *stemma*.

Kurt Weitzmann, professor of art history at Princeton University, pioneered applying this same approach to iconography: comparing icons, noting the distinguishing features (the variants) in the midst of the similarities, and arranging them in a likely sequence. This can be done only by making many, many comparisons. The more comparisons you are able to make, the more secure you can be about assigning probable dates and places of origin.

The work that Weitzmann did here at Sinai was essential to his development of this theory, since we have icons covering such a long span of time, and without breaks in the order. It was Weitzmann who declared that the encaustic icon of Christ must be dated to the sixth century, that such a high order of icon painting could have come only from Constantinople, and that it must have been an imperial gift to the monastery at the time of its foundation by the emperor Justinian. He was able to point to comparable examples to defend this dating and provenance. I think that all scholars since then have accepted his dating of this icon.

For the last fifteen hundred years, the Sinai Christ has been carefully preserved at St. Catherine's, arguably one of the most spiritually potent sites in world history, standing as it does at the foot of Mount Sinai. According to tradition, the location of this monastery is where God spoke to Moses from the burning bush (Exod. 3:1–2). And this was the mountain on which he received the Ten Commandments. As one of the few icons dating from before the period of iconoclasm (730–787 and 814–843), it is of inestimable value to art historians.

The simplicity of its subject matter—the face of Christ—should not blind us to its profundity, even ineffability. In contemplating this icon, we are forced to wrestle with some of the deepest questions in the Christian discourse. How can the dual nature of Jesus Christ, in his role as both God and man, be portrayed in this world? This icon is the most powerful example of the union of symbolism and historical truth that forms the basis for all sacred art in the culture of Eastern-rite Christianity. This particular variation of the iconographic subject of the Savior is known as the Pantocrator—the ruler of the universe, quite literally "Lord of All."

Traditionally, Pantocrator icons look down on the worshiper from inside the highest dome of an Orthodox church. They also appear on the icon screen at the front of the church, which separates the altar area from the main body of the church. These two locations are the most important spaces in the church and therefore are the only appropriate places for "Christ, Lord of All."

In the architectural layout of churches, as in all aspects of Orthodox art, form follows function. Thus the more important the event or person depicted, the higher up in the physical space of the church it appears. The invariable order that underlies the organization of all of the frescos and icons gracing the walls of Orthodox churches worldwide will be the subject of chapter 7. At this point, suffice it to say that both the architecture and the interior decoration of any Orthodox church are one continuous theological statement writ large. And since the Pantocrator rules over all, his image appears on the highest point in the church.

While explaining the centrality of Christ might seem redundant to the Western reader, the literary and graphic imagery through which this centrality is expressed developed differently in the West and in the East. If we look at the sculptures on the outside of medieval churches and cathedrals in England and France, we may see the figure of Christ sitting on a throne, known to art historians as Christ in Majesty. This image is clearly related to the Pantocrator icon of the East. However, by the fourteenth century, interest in this particular image waned in the West. It was replaced by the Crucifixion, the Pieta, and the Madonna and Child as the most popular depictions of the Savior.

Humanism, which was a major intellectual force in Renaissance Europe, naturally favored an intellectually accessible depiction of Christ, as either a lovely infant or as the suffering Everyman on the road to Calvary and the crucifixion. For Eastern-rite Christians, however, even today Christ Pantocrator remains one of the most popular iconographic subjects. In fact, for the Orthodox bride and groom, the traditional wedding present from their parents remains the two indispensable icons without which it is deemed impossible to start a new household: the Theotokos and Child, and Christ Pantocrator.

Questions That Shook the Church

For Byzantine Christians during the time when the Sinai Savior was painted, the entire content of religious life depended on how the question "Who is Jesus Christ?" was answered. Debates between the Orthodox church proper and various factions, including the Monophysites, the Monotheletes, and the Monoenergists—each of which understood the implications of Christ's incarnation in different ways—reached a climax in the fifth century.

In 451, in the Byzantine city of Chalcedon, the leaders of the Christian church, both East and West, defined the outer limits of permissible speculation about the nature of Christ and the mystery of his incarnation. The consequent belief embraced by the church was that humanity and divinity were mingled in the nature of Christ. As we've seen, St. Athanasius' doctrine of deification became the centerpiece of the view: "Christ became man so that man could become God." The material aspect of Christ was thus recognized as being not only fully expressible but in fact worthy of emulation.

Man's deification as an important facet of the Sinai Christ's overall meaning becomes apparent when we consider the church where this icon hangs. St. Catherine's Monastery is dedicated to the Transfiguration of our Lord. Beneath the high altar, the holiest spot in this church, are what many Christians believe to be the remains of the burning bush through which Moses heard the voice of God. The imagery of the Transfiguration theme imbued the original setting for this icon and doubtlessly affected the way it was perceived by the faithful—the chasm between Creator and creation having been bridged by Christ.

While gazing at the Sinai Pantocrator, we should never forget that the physical image of Christ is recognized by the Orthodox church as a channel through which humankind may draw nearer to God, enabling us to return to the state of grace and incorruptibility enjoyed by Adam and Eve before the fall. Of course—and this point is reiterated time and again—it is not simply flesh but the holy flesh of the Lord that is represented in icons and that should be emulated by man. As Theodore the Studite, a seventh-century desert father, explains, "The representation of Christ is not in the likeness of a corruptible man, which is disapproved of by the apostles, but as he himself said earlier, it is in the likeness of the incorruptible man, but incorruptible precisely because he is not simply a man but God who became man."

Christ is called the "last Adam" (1 Cor. 15:45), the new archetype through whom all of creation, headed by man, will return to its true state, which is the state of grace or harmony with God. This is why the Orthodox worshiper cannot accept the realism or even naturalism of some Western depictions of the Savior, such as Rubens' *Descent from the Cross*, in which Christ's already decaying body is being lifted off the cross by Joseph of Arimathea, John, and Mary.

The assertion of the physical reality of Christ's presence on earth also rejected the metaphoric or symbolic approach to Christ's nature advocated by certain churchmen from Egypt, chief among them Origen. These led to depictions of Christ as the Good Shepherd, a lamb, a fish, a vine, or even as Orpheus with a lyre in his hand surrounded by animals. The Council of 553, which condemned Origen and his followers, was a turning point in Christian theology, reiterating the biblical view of creation, based on a Christ grounded in space and time and on a view of history as a linear progression leading to the second coming.

Consequently, symbolic and metaphoric depictions of Christ rapidly fell from favor. These symbolic images can be found on the most ancient monuments of Christian art, among them the catacombs, and also appear as literary tropes in some of the patristic writings. At the same time, a quickening of interest in historically based likenesses of Christ was taking place. It was during this period that the icon of the Sinai Christ first appeared.

Rome's Church of St. Pudentia, a late fourth-century edifice, provides an interesting illustration of these changes in the image of Christ. The mosaic in the apse depicts the Church of the Old Testament and the Church of the New Testament in the form of allegorical female figures. These are dominated by the figure of Christ, dressed in Roman senatorial robes and surrounded by his disciples, likewise attired. Christ is clean shaven, in the Roman fashion, following the prototype of the Good Shepherd and Orpheus.

Two hundred years later, images of a clean-shaven Christ are few. And the same desire for historicity that made the clean-shaven Christ unacceptable also prompted an interest in images of Christ based on the miraculous imprinting of his face, such as the Mandylion, commonly known by the name Holy Visage icons.

Before the fifth century, no authors mention the image of the Holy Visage. Evagrius (sixth century) first speaks of it in his *Ecclesiastical History*, in which he calls the portrait of Christ imprinted on a piece of linen "the icon made by God." In the traditional story, King Abgar, a leper, was the ruler of a small country between the Tigris and Euphrates rivers. He had a servant named Hannan, whom he sent to Christ with a letter in which the king asked Jesus to come to Edessa, his capital city, to cure him of his disease. Hannan was a painter, and in case Christ refused to go, he was instructed to paint an image of Christ and return with that to the king.

Hannan encountered great difficulties in accomplishing this mission; the vast crowds kept him at a distance. Even when the painter climbed a tree, he could not succeed in making Christ's portrait because "of the indescribable glory of his face which was changing through grace," in the words of the liturgical reading for August 16—the Holy Visage or Mandylion feast day.

Seeing that Hannan wanted to paint his portrait, Christ asked for some water. He washed his face and wiped it with a linen towel, on which his features remained imprinted. This Christ gave to Hannan. The original piece of linen on which the face of the Lord was imprinted was kept in Edessa until 944 CE, when it was taken to Constantinople. After the crusaders sacked the Byzantine capital in 1204, all traces of this relic were lost. Interestingly enough, the Shroud of Turin has been carbon-dated from approximately the same time period, the thirteenth century, although some researchers dispute that date.

Other stories about the history of Christ's portraits abound. Father Justin writes,

> Eusebius, Bishop of Caesarea, was a close friend of the Emperor Constantine, who put an end to the Roman persecutions. Eusebius wrote a very important Church History. Many of the texts he quoted have since been lost, and we only have the quotations that were made by Eusebius.
>
> He mentions that the woman with an issue of blood who was healed by Christ, out of gratitude for her healing, made a statue of Christ standing and blessing her, and herself kneeling before Him and looking up to him in gratitude. We know that this statue remained in existence until it was deliberately destroyed by Julian the Apostate. Thus, one who had known Christ had a likeness of Him made, and this remained in existence for over three centuries.

Eusebius also mentions having seen portraits of the Apostles painted on wood panels. This is the more significant, in that he himself had an aversion to images. We know that many in the early Church did, because of the abundance of pagan statues and paintings. But as the threat of paganism subsided, the likenesses of Christ and the Apostles and Saints that had been preserved from early times became more important in the Church.

We also know that there was a highly developed tradition of portraiture in the Roman Empire. In every court [i.e., palace], there was a painting or statue of the Emperor, which was honoured as if the Emperor himself were present in the court. This honour depended on the faithfulness of the likeness to the prototype. All of this argues for the ability of artists at that time to capture likenesses faithfully, and for these likenesses to be carefully preserved, both the original, and any copies made deriving from them.

These topics are battlefields, and they are scarred with the many wars that have been fought on them. But I think that there is less antipathy in our times than there has been in times past, and perhaps this will allow a more reasoned and balanced review of these questions.

In the sixth century, interest in the Holy Visage was an important element in the spread of Savior icons, such as the Sinai Christ, throughout Byzantium. This world, however, was fast approaching a period of extreme crisis. Despite an outward appearance of cultural and political unity, the Byzantine Empire was rife with schism. The Byzantine state involved itself in enforcing the outcome of the decisions of the first six ecumenical church councils. Many of the theological and administrative issues that were raised at these councils were not resolved. Instead, they went underground and festered, ready to erupt at any time.

The people of this empire, which stretched from parts of present-day Bulgaria through all of Asia Minor and the modern Mideast, including Egypt and Libya, were all nominally Christian. However, their native pre-Christian religious traditions divided them into two camps, culturally speaking. The descendents of people who participated in a culture influenced by classical Greece were amenable to using images in worship, while the non-Greeks disliked images, associating them with paganism.

In the seventh century, the Muslim Arabs conquered Syria and Palestine, and in 717 they besieged Constantinople. Under the pressure of a triumphant Islam, differences in attitudes toward icon veneration reemerged and hardened. The Muslims' strict rejection of graven images spoke to the long-suppressed doubts concerning the propriety of icons among many Byzantine citizens. The Arabs were driven back out of Asia Minor by Emperor Leo III, who was himself a non-Greek of Armenian origin. In 730, the emperor published a decree, approved by the imperial senate, forbidding the veneration of icons in the Byzantine Empire. Patriarch St. Germanus refused to sign this decree, as did Pope St. Gregory II in Rome. Germanus demanded that an ecumenical council be called. Leo III deposed the patriarch and replaced him with an iconoclast.

The first iconoclastic act, by order of the emperor, was to destroy an icon of Christ (probably also of the Pantocrator type) that hung above one of the imperial palace gates. The demolition of this icon provoked a popular uprising, which was harshly suppressed. Christian blood flowed, and tens of thousands of icons were destroyed. Crumbling under the strain of foreign invasion and civil war, Byzantine society broke apart into two warring factions: the iconodules or "icon lovers," and the iconoclasts or "icon destroyers." Difficult as it may be for us today to envision killing over disparate views about icons, this was a horribly real and bloody schism.

It should be noted here that the iconoclasts did not reject all figurative art *per se*; on the contrary they decorated both palaces and churches with flowers, birds, landscapes, and animal figures, in the Hellenistic artistic tradition. They also tolerated nonfigurative religious art: the cross as a geometric form without Christ's figure was often used in iconoclastic decorative schemes. The only symbolic representation of Christ that they unanimously found acceptable, however, was the Eucharist itself. Every other image was deemed idolatrous and destroyed, including all images of the Virgin Mary and the saints.

Interestingly, it was outside the borders of the Byzantine Empire, in the lands recently conquered by the armies of Islam, where the chief defender of the icon appeared. Immediately after the 730 decree, a highly educated civil servant of the caliph, known as John of Damascus (he was born in Damascus), responded with the first of his three treatises, *In Defense of the Holy Icons*. St. John lived in political isolation from Constantinople, under the Muslim caliphate. He was thus spared the official persecution suffered by his Orthodox brethren within the political boundaries of Byzantium and could compose his treatises in relative peace. His treatises remain, down to the present, the definitive texts concerning the theological meaning of icons in the Orthodox faith.

St. John of Damascus' writings became the theological cornerstone for the Seventh Ecumenical Council, called into session by Empress Irene in 787, to address the icon issue. This council reestablished the veneration of icons as a basic tenet of the Orthodox faith. The main point—summarized—was that with the incarnation, a decisive and eternal change took place in the relationship between God and material creation. Matter became sanctified, and the opposition between matter and spirit was no longer valid. To restate St. John's First Oration, "I do not worship matter, but I worship the Creator of matter who became matter for my sake . . . and who, through matter, accomplished my salvation. Never will I cease to honor the matter which brought about my salvation."

114

Christ, Ruler of All

The Sinai Christ was painted using the encaustic technique. *Encaustic* means "painting with heat" and refers to the early art of painting with pigments of various colors that have been suspended in melted beeswax and then applied to the canvas with a spatula. It is interesting to note that from the first century CE through the early Byzantine period, the custom in Egypt was to bury those who could afford it in mummy cases decorated with encaustic or hot wax portraits of the deceased. Beeswax was considered an especially pure and spiritually beneficial substance. Even in the present day, Orthodox churches will not use any other material for their candles. Beeswax is, therefore, quite appropriate for use on icons.

About the icon's coloration, Father Justin says, "In classical times, it was felt that if a painting had too many colors, it lost its gravity. The most esteemed paintings were painted with four colors: white (lead oxide), ochre, red (both earth pigments), and black (vine black, obtained from converting grapevines into charcoal—when mixed with white, this forms a blue-gray color). You see exactly these colors, and no more (apart from the gold leaf), on the Sinai icon of Christ."

In the Sinai Pantocrator icon, Christ is robed in what appears to be a royal tunic. In his left hand he holds a jewel-studded Gospel. His right hand is raised in blessing; two fingers are raised, symbolizing his dual nature, and the other three folded down, symbolizing the Trinity. A golden nimbus encircles his head, representing the divine energy or grace that streams from him. The Gospel is closed. It was only during the fourteenth century, when a much more text-oriented public hovered on the brink of the Gutenburg printing revolution, that icons of this type begin to depict the Gospel standing wide open on the Savior's knee, with the words of a biblical passage written on its pages.

As we have seen, the features on Jesus' face are uneven, indicating the balance between justice and mercy. One eye is said to reflect the judgment of God; the other to reflect his forgiveness, causing some to call images like this one Christ of the Angry Eye.

Icons and Ancient Landscapes

It is interesting to think about the impact of the Sinai landscape on the portrayal of nature in icons. Although they do not appear in the Sinai Christ, sharp, sculpted cliffs, sandy-colored earth, stunted and gnarled trees predominate images of the natural world in Orthodox icons prior to eighteenth-century Westernization. What is the reason for this strange phenomenon? Perhaps it is because the mountainous and barren landscape of Mount Sinai was the prototype for iconographers both on the Sinai Peninsula and thousands of miles away. A whole "Sinaitic school" came into existence during the reign of Emperor Justinian I (527–565 CE). Paradoxically, due to the remoteness and inaccessibility of the monastery, it came to wield a decisive influence in the development of post-iconoclastic iconography worldwide.

For centuries, Mount Sinai was a haven for desert monks and hermits. A chapel, erected at the foot of Mount Sinai sometime in the fourth century, is dedicated to the Virgin as "the burning bush." This parallel connects the Exodus story with the Virgin's bearing within her human body the Second Person of the Trinity, "the fire that did not consume her."

Emperor Justinian ordered a fortification built in the sixth century to secure Sinai's monastic communities from occasional raids by desert nomads. Sometime between 548 and 565 CE, the Basilica of the Transfiguration replaced the Burning Bush Chapel. The Monastery of St. Catherine thus became an isolated stronghold approximately the size of a city block, with its own church, dormitories, and workshops. Monks from all over the Byzantine world came to its doors.

When the iconoclast movement swept through the Byzantine Empire, the monks in St. Catherine's remained true to Orthodoxy and did not destroy any of their icons, including the Sinai Christ. Thus, the monastery became one of the world's richest depositories of ancient icons and manuscripts. It was after visiting the Monastery of St. Catherine that German scholar Herman Tischendorff returned to Europe in 1840 with the Codex Sinaiaticus in his knapsack. This is still the world's oldest existing copy of the New Testament, dating back to the fourth century. While Tischendorff claimed to have found the precious manuscript in a pile of kindling, waiting to be burned by the monks for fuel, the actual story is shrouded in contradictory accounts.

The present-day monks of St. Catherine's Monastery seem convinced that Tischendorff stole their precious manuscript, after plying the monastery librarian with alcohol. This story is related by British author William Dalrymple in his fascinating book on the Christians of the Middle East, *From the Holy Mountain*. Today, the Monastery of St. Catherine and the Basilica of the Transfiguration are among the finest surviving examples of Byzantine architecture. Both have been named UNESCO World Heritage Sites. The Codex Sinaiaticus is in the British Library.

The Abandoned Cradle of Christianity

St. John of Damascus brings us to a historical subject not well known to Western Christians but quite important for understanding the development of Orthodox iconography: the role of the Arabs in the world of Eastern Christianity. It seems very likely the Sinai Christ was actually painted within the confines of St. Catherine's Monastery, but it is equally probable that its author was an Egyptian Christian.

The Christian Middle East today is little more than a phantom. Instead of the millions of Christians who once lived there, mere thousands remain, surrounded by a sea of Islam. This should not blind us to the fact that in the early and middle years of the Byzantine Empire, the Middle East was the spiritual and intellectual backbone of the Orthodox Christian Empire. The desert fathers who made their way into the Egyptian and Palestinian wilderness and to Mount Sinai codified, through word and deed, the early Christian ideal of an ascetic, noninstitutionalized monasticism.

Intellectually, Alexandria and Antioch were the two great centers for the study of theology right up to their capture by the Muslim armies in the seventh century. Even after the subjugation of the Christian population to Muslim suzerainty, the influence of this population continued to be felt in Byzantium proper, as witnessed by the theological career of St. John of Damascus. It should be noted that after writing his famous treatises in defense of icons, St. John withdrew from the caliph's court and went to a Palestinian monastery, St. Sabbaas, located in the desert not far from Jerusalem. There he ended his days in peace and prayer.

The comparative ease with which the Muslim invaders captured and subdued much of the Middle Eastern area of the Byzantine Empire was the result, in part, of the relative tolerance that Islam extended to the other two "people of the book," Jews and Christians. While condemned to a second-class civic existence, both groups were free to worship in any way they saw fit. This attitude was a welcome change from the government-sponsored persecution of religious heterogeneity that fueled the iconoclast persecutions of Orthodox Christians and vice versa.

In the summer of 646, the Arab general Amr recaptured Alexandria. In response, the Monophysite Christian (Coptic) population of the city, led by their patriarch, willingly ratified their terms of surrender. Perhaps the marginalized Monophysite believers preferred the Arab yoke to that of the Byzantines, who continued forcefully to impose the Chalcedonian definition of Christ's manhood on their fellow citizens to the bitter end.

But it was not until the twentieth century that the scourge of nationalism finally sounded the death knell for Christians in the Middle East. First came the genocide of Armenia's Christian population by the Ottoman government in 1915. Then, after 1956, Nasser's nationalistic government confiscated the property of all non-Egyptians, among them Orthodox Greeks and Armenian Christians who had lived in Egypt from the time of the Roman Empire. Then began the civil war in Lebanon, during which tens of thousands of Christians emigrated in the 1970s. Christian footprints in the desert sands are rapidly vanishing. Today, there is not a single Christian church in the ancient city of Edessa, now known by the name of Urfa. The town where, for centuries, the Holy Visage was kept seems to have completely forgotten its Christian past.

But elsewhere, there are those who still remember, even in such remote places as Mount Sinai. In the words of theologian Christof von Schonburn in his work *L'Icone du Christ, Fonedements Theologiques*, "The Christological debates lasted for centuries. During all those years the Church never ceased to confess the mystery revealed and sealed in the Holy Face of Jesus Christ, the consubstantial image of the Father. . . . After viewing these terrible distressing struggles around the true confession of Christ, our gaze stops and settles on an image that is silent and serene: the icon of Christ."

The icon of the Sinai Christ, like any icon of Jesus Christ Pantocrator, represents the Son of God as a heavenly personage. It reminds me of the reality that lies beyond it, a powerful reality which gives it its name and its meaning.

119

My own little reproduction of the Sinai icon has sometimes been left in a drawer for weeks or has gathered dust on a shelf, more or less forgotten. Eventually I've rediscovered it, dusted it off, admired it, set it near a candle, and absorbed its unique beauty and meaning. Unquestionably, apart from the one it represents, it is virtually worthless.

It occurs to me, however, that I, too, am made in the image of God and am therefore myself an icon in the world. No matter where I go or what circumstances I encounter, my value lies in the one whose image is imprinted upon my being. Whether I am battered or beautiful, old or modern, colorful or neutral, original or a copy of an original, I remain an icon, bearing in my human nature the image of Christ.

As with any icon, some people will see me only as a material presence. Others may catch a glimpse of something unusual or "spiritual" about me. A few will think I am archaic and outdated. One or two may look for a kind of power in me that I cannot offer. Some will say that I am worthless. Some will imagine that I have performed a miracle. It is my prayer that now and then, someone will recognize the image of Christ in me and will look through me like a window— opaque and tarnished and dusty as I am—and will fix their eyes on the realities of heaven.

Notes

. . . *have accepted his dating of this icon.* Father Justin, curator at the Monastery of St. Catherine in Sinai, Egypt, interview with Lela Gilbert, October 28–30, 2003.

. . . *but God who became man.* Daniel B. Clendenin, ed., *Eastern Orthodox Theology: A Contemporary Reader* (Grand Rapids: Baker, 1995), 43.

... *This Christ gave to Hannan.* Leonid Ouspensky, *Theology of the Icon*, vol. 1, tr. Anthony Gythiel and Elizabeth Meyendorff (Crestwood, NY: St. Vladimir's Seminary Press, 1992), 51.

... *reasoned and balanced review of these questions.* Father Justin, curator at the Monastery of St. Catherine in Sinai, Egypt, interview, October 28–30, 2003.

... *which brought about my salvation.* John of Damascus, *On the Divine Images*, Second Apology, chap. 14.

... *to the bitter end.* William Dalrymple, *From the Holy Mountain: A Journey among Christians of the Middle East* (New York: Henry Holt, 1997), 429.

... *the icon of Christ.* Ouspensky, *Theology of the Icon*, vol. 1, 148.

7

The Church

Where God Dwells among Men

Then I heard every creature in heaven and on earth and under
the earth and on the sea, and all that is in them, singing:
  "To him who sits on the throne and to the Lamb
  be praise and honor and glory and power,
  for ever and ever!"

—Revelation 5:13

*A friend and I were sightseeing in Kiev when our driver
stopped in front of the Cathedral of St. Vladimir. We looked
at each other, shrugged, and compliantly got out of the car.
We hadn't meant to attend church that Sunday. And since*

we had been told that Orthodoxy was all but dead in that part of the world—perhaps wishful thinking on the part of some missionary-minded traveling companions—we assumed that if we went into St. Vladimir's, there would be but a handful of little old babushkas praying.

Nothing could have been farther from the truth. To our amazement, the cathedral was packed with worshipers of all ages. Some stood, while many others were on their knees. There were no seats; everyone either stood or kneeled. We had entered midservice, but it didn't matter. No one noticed us save one woman, who shook her finger silently at the sight of my camera. I self-consciously nodded and dropped it into my handbag.

There was so much happening, and it was so foreign, that for a moment or two, it was difficult to focus. Then a pure tenor voice cut through the rustling sounds around us. Was the singer a priest or a cantor? I had no idea, but his solo was suddenly answered by a choir somewhere above, its voice so powerful, so rich in harmony, so pure in tone that it instantly brought tears to my eyes.

The church was ablaze with candlelight. Every icon, and there seemed to be dozens of them, was surrounded by a glowing aura of slender, amber candles. Countless bouquets of roses and other summer flowers, offerings from the myriad worshipers, blended their scents with clouds of incense. The warm air was heavy with fragrance.

At a small counter, unobtrusively placed near the doorway, candles were sold for a few cents each. I knew they represented prayers, and as usual, I needed more than my share. Not sure why I continued to feel tearful, I lit them from already burning wicks and randomly set them in front of icons. In my conscious mind, I had no idea what I was doing; my spirit seemed to have a mind of its own. I couldn't grasp a word of the haunting liturgy, although I was vaguely able to follow, since it seemed similar to the order of the Episcopal prayer book.

We were surrounded by vibrant images of Christ's life and death, of vast heavenly hosts, of beloved Bible stories. The music was unearthly and continued to pierce to the heart. The humility of those around me was compelling. But most important of all—for me at least—somewhere in the midst of such foreign and bewildering ceremony, I somehow managed to stop thinking, to stop analyzing, to stop comparing. I forgot myself completely and was absorbed into a unity of worship unlike anything I had experienced before.

The Church is the fourth dimension through which we catch a glimpse of eternity, the channel by which the divine energy of God enters into our three-dimensional world.

There are many reasons to treasure the world's Orthodox churches—historical reasons, artistic reasons, even reasons of national symbolism. But the primary function of any Orthodox shrine is to serve as the physical space in which believers participate in the celebration of the Eucharist. This is in response to the words of the Savior: "For where two or three come together in my name, there am I with them" (Matt. 18:20). Wherever Christian believers gather, Christ is present. And in Orthodox worship, we are invited into a heavenly environment to be with him.

The church is the House of Wisdom where the Logos abides, the place of the eternal, life-giving sacrifice: "Wisdom hath builded her house, she hath hewn out her seven pillars: She hath killed her beasts; she hath mingled her wine; she hath also furnished her table.... She crieth upon the highest places of the city, ... 'come, eat of my bread, and drink of the wine which I have mingled'" (Prov. 9:1–5 KJV).

Standing between Two Worlds

The church, as the site of the Divine Liturgy, is a paradox. It is a place with physical dimensions, painted a certain color, decorated with certain elements that are more or less pleasing to the eye. But it is also an interstice, a fragment of eternity not bound by our understanding of space and time. During the reenactment of and participation in Christ's sacrifice and resurrection, there is no "then" and no "now," no "mine" and no "yours," no "inside" and no "outside." All categories of perception are suspended in the face of eternity.

In Orthodox worship, the church ceiling becomes the vault of heaven. The saints painted on the pillars of the church stand among the worshipers, shouldering our burdens as well as their own, keeping the spiritual edifice of the church from collapsing under the heavy doubt of our secular age. Clouds of incense float by, reminiscent of the clouds that appeared as the firmament was divided from the waters during creation. The candles flickering everywhere embody the prayers of the faithful—the prayers of the living for the dead, and the prayers of the dead for the living, all offered in community. Angelic hymns sung both by an earthly choir and its celestial counterpart rise in a crescendo of beauty. At times, the sound seems to echo from the heavens. At other times, it dies away in a sigh at the foot of the cross.

This feeling of communion and community creates, at least in part, the unique attraction of the Orthodox worship and liturgy. It is community unmarred by the fatal fissures of time or space. It is communion among all creatures—living and dead, saint and sinner, and most important, Creator and creation. To paraphrase the words of Archimandrite Vasileos, "The liturgy addresses itself to human nature universally, to humankind's thirst for something beyond."

Special edifices were not required for the gatherings of the first Christians. Beneath the sidewalks of present-day Rome lie the ruins of many ancient buildings, such as laundries and grain storehouses, adapted by Christians as gathering places for their meetings. Later, when special edifices dedicated to Christian worship were built, they were constructed to reflect the glory of the heavenly kingdom. The figure of Christ Pantocrator, ruler of all, presided over these early Orthodox churches—literally and figuratively—in their attempt to depict a transfigured reality.

The first official history of the Kievan state, known as *The Primary Chronicle*, was written between 1040 and 1188. It contains an account of the conversion of the Kievan Rus' to Byzantine Christianity. As we saw in chapter 2, this took place during the reign of Prince (later Saint) Vladimir in 988, when the prince's envoys went to Constantinople and attended a service in the Hagia Sophia, the most glorious church in Christendom at the time. They returned extolling the splendor of the worship there.

Whether apocryphal or not, the story gives centrality to aesthetic beauty in the Christian experience as a characteristic of Orthodoxy, and it remains true to the present day. Orthodox Christians believe that beauty is the seal and sign of the Creator. And so the interior of the Orthodox church, with its rich imagery, sweet-smelling incense, and sublime choral music, serves to commemorate and celebrate the Creator's presence in this world as well as in the next.

Fixed Rules of Order

In earlier chapters, we discussed the theological and philosophical influences that underlie the use of icons or images in the context of the Orthodox liturgy. It might be useful at this point, however, before we examine the spatial organization of an Orthodox shrine, to reiterate the premise behind this usage.

For the Orthodox, the church is the body of Christ, the sign of God's providential wisdom as manifested here on earth. Since the Christian God is a living God, all believers, whether living or dead, are part of Christ's body. Thus the Orthodox faithful believe that the images, or icons, not only of Christ but of the Theotokos and the saints and angels have a rightful place on the walls of Wisdom's house. The people represented by the icons serve both as vital examples of Christian virtue and as advocates for those still living on earth, interceding for us before the throne of God.

An Orthodox church building functions as the physical model of the transcendental cosmos. Its interior space is the means by which theological truths are made manifest. There should never be dissonance between a church's architectural integrity and the spiritual meaning within its walls. It bears repeating: in an Orthodox church, form always follows function.

The decorative program of frescos and icons is organized according to fixed rules. The more important the subject, the higher it is placed within the confines of the church. And the more central the theological concept depicted, the closer it is placed to the midpoint of the spatial plane on which it is portrayed.

The curve of the domed ceiling represents the vaults of heaven. Figures of the transfigured Christ, of the Theotokos in her heavenly glory, and of the angels are found in this space. Midway down the walls, and closer to the earthly existence of the congregation, which stands praying on the floor of the church, the walls are covered with frescos depicting the major events of Christ's life

128

on earth, as well as those of the particular saint or feast day to which the shrine is dedicated. Lit candles, as symbols of prayers rising to heaven, light the interior of the shrine.

Because the parishioners feel themselves to be standing before the face of the King of Kings, they often choose not to sit. This is why, traditionally, there are no pews to break up and organize the interior spaces of the church. Only a few seats in the back acknowledge the realities of the flesh's frailties and the burdens of old age and illness.

From the Outside Looking In

Historically, the exterior form of Orthodox church buildings has followed one of several theologically inspired symbolic prototypes. Sometimes it is designed as a symmetrical cross, with two evenly intersecting wings—a sign of faith in the crucified Christ. Sometimes the structure is oblong or rectangular, which alludes to the church as a ship that will convey the faithful through life's stormy seas to the safe haven of the kingdom of heaven. And sometimes it is designed as a circle, symbolically representing eternity. Orthodox churches are oriented on an east-west axis, with the main entrance on the west and the altar facing east, since the sun, seen symbolically as Christ, the "Sun of Righteousness," rises in the east.

Many Orthodox churches are topped with domes or cupolas, which speak of the celestial realm stretching out over our earthly existence. Cupolas come in symbolic numerical groupings; one (God's unity), two (divinity and humanity of Christ), three (the Trinity), four (the evangelists), twelve (the apostles), as well as other combinations.

A peculiar feature of Orthodox churches built in Russia, or following the Russian style, is the onion-shaped dome. There are several theories as to why this particular architectural feature evolved. It first appeared in the lands of Muscovite Russia, in the post-Tatar period. Some historians claim that the onion shapes are an adaptation of the Byzantine cupola to the snowy climate of northern Russian; the concave curves of the onion shape simply keep snow from accumulating on the church roof during the long winter months. Others say they are a sign of Asian cultural influence. Still others believe that these domes are actually flame shaped and, like lit candles, symbolize the prayers of the saints rising toward heaven.

Each cupola is crowned with a cross. These crosses can be found in various shapes, but among the most familiar are the Greek cross, which consists of two intersecting bars of equal length, and the Russian cross, which consists of three bars and a slanted footboard at the bottom. The latter is a more concrete depiction of the implement of crucifixion, with a direct reference to the signboard on which was written in Hebrew, Latin, and Greek, "Jesus of Nazareth, the King of the Jews" (John 19:19). The slanted footboard, pointing upward to the right, is a reminder of the repentant thief, crucified on Jesus' right, who was promised a place in paradise (Luke 23).

Form, Function, and Theology in Color

The interior of an Orthodox church is divided into three parts: the narthex or vestibule, the nave or main body of the church, and the altar, typically separated from the nave by a screen of icons known as the iconostasis.

In the early centuries of the Christian church, when there were many adult converts, the catechumens (those under instruction in the Christian faith in preparation for baptism) stood in the vestibule. This was also the area for penitents—women and men who had already been baptized but who, due to some transgression, were deemed unworthy of participation in the communion.

The counter or stand where the congregation buys candles, if it is located in the church at all, must be located in the narthex.

The nave, or the central part of the church, stretches out into a wide open area. Typically, at its center, flanked by candlestands, is a stand carrying the icon of the saint's day or feast day that is being commemorated on a particular Sunday. On the far right corner of the nave stands a life-sized crucifix, and in front of it is another candlestand, whose candles symbolize the prayers for the dead. At the farthest eastern end of the nave is a raised platform; its central part is called the *ambon*, from the Greek word meaning "to go up." This is the place for the sacred eucharistic ritual. Above it towers the screen of the iconostasis, whose complex combination of imagery is a literal depiction of the mystery behind the sacrament of Holy Communion.

The iconostasis is the most prominent architectural feature in the interior of an Orthodox church. It is made up of several tiers of icons, serving as screens between the altar and the nave. These screens have existed in Christian churches from ancient times. Church fathers, among them St. Gregory the Theologian and St. John Chrysostom, as well as early church historian Eusebius, all mention screens in their writings.

Over the centuries, the form and height of the original altar screens have varied. Sometimes they were chest-high balustrades, while in other shrines they were higher latticed screens. In early historic descriptions, a curtain hangs on the interior side of the screen closest to the sanctuary, which is drawn open or closed depending on the particular moment in the church service. Clearly this curtain is a reference to the curtain in the ancient Jerusalem temple. Down to the present day, it continues to function as a marker in the course of the Orthodox service: the most important moments in the liturgy take place when the curtain is open to the altar.

The iconostasis serves as a boundary between two worlds, the divine and the human, the transitory and the eternal. As a boundary—and this is a very important point—the iconostasis both divides and unites. While physically shielding the sacred mysteries of the altar from all eyes save those of the clerics performing them, it also reflects a state of the universe in which the contradictions between Creator and creature, humanity and nature are overcome and reconciled. It is a map or guide pointing out the key landmarks on the path of reconciliation.

A closer look at an iconostasis, such as the one at the Russian Orthodox Cathedral of St. John the Baptist in Washington, D.C., reveals four rows of icons—a fairly common number in Orthodox churches—and these are organized in a specific way.

The bottom row of icons, closest to the believers, is known as the local row, since it includes icons specific to the particular local church. It is interrupted by two sets of doors, the royal doors in the center of the row, and two side doors, known as deacon's doors. The royal doors are central to the row, and on them are placed icons of the four evangelists, who have conveyed to us the texts central to Christian salvation. The Eucharist is carried out through these doors. At their center is an image of the Annunciation, since this event was the necessary prelude to humankind's salvation. Above the royal doors, an icon of the Last Supper is placed to announce that the Eucharist, the sacrament Christ first instituted the night before his death, is celebrated on the altar beyond. At either side of the royal doors are placed an icon of the Savior (to the right) and of the Mother of God (to the left).

The next row is the Deisis row, named for the central composition, which is the Theotokos and St. John the Baptist standing in prayerful supplication before the figure of Christ Enthroned. The word *deisis* means "prayer," and this row is a depiction of the intercessory function of the Mother of God and St. John. The rest of the row is taken up with other figures, archangels, and saints who also intercede for humankind before the throne of God. All of the figures rhythmically echo one another in their common movement, bowing and raising their arms in supplication before the Lord sitting on his throne.

The third row of the iconostasis is that of the holy days, which, depending on the width of the screen, depicts all or most of the twelve major feast days of the Orthodox calendar. Six of these are feast days dedicated to the Lord: Nativity, Presentation at the Temple, Epiphany, Transfiguration, Entry into Jerusalem, and Ascension. Four are dedicated to the Virgin: her Birth, Presentation at the Temple, Annunciation, and Dormition. The central two icons in this row are of the Crucifixion and the Resurrection, the central feast days in the Orthodox calendar year.

The last row, the Prophets, crowns the four-tiered iconostasis. It consists of images of Old Testament prophets with scrolls in their hands, on which are written their prophecies concerning the divine incarnation. This row depicts the church of the Old Testament as both a premonition and the fulfillment of the New Testament. David and Solomon, Zachariah and Ezekiel, Moses and Haggai, Samuel and Elias, Nahum and Malachi, Daniel and Elisha, and Habakkuk are arranged to the right and to the left of an image of the Theotokos as Our Lady of the Sign. The Theotokos, and Christ within her as the literal fulfillment of their prophecies, is placed at the center of the prophets. Once again, decorative form follows theological function.

Finally, at the very top of the iconostasis stands the Holy Cross upon which the Lord was crucified. This is the culminating point of the economy of salvation.

The altar that lies beyond the iconostasis is a sacrosanct area, set aside for those who perform the Divine Liturgy. Normally, people not consecrated to the service of the church are not permitted to enter. In this, the Orthodox church has remained true to the service culture of the Old Testament temple in Jerusalem, which is the prototype of the Christian church service.

Occupying the central place in the altar is the holy table, representing the throne of God. This is where the preparations for the Eucharist take place. Just as the cross is the focal point of the salvation story, the sacramental mystery of the Eucharist lies at the heart of Orthodox worship.

Impressions of a Sunday Service

A Western visitor to an Orthodox service encounters an unfamiliar, perhaps briefly confusing, sensory realm. The first impression may well be one of subdued but joyful chaos, punctuated by periods of intense attention. Due to the absence of pews or chairs, each member of the congregation in the nave and the narthex is free to worship in his or her own fashion. Historians tell us that this is not an anomaly but the arrangement followed even by Western Christian churches until the fourteenth century, when pews first started coming into fashion.

The scene in a typical Orthodox church seems quite medieval to a person with modern sensibilities and expectations of standardized and orderly behavior in a house of worship. But this in no way detracts from the impression of devout religiosity. Some people are putting candles in the candlestands and praying ardently before one or another of the icons that hang on the church walls. Others are venerating the feast day icon in the middle of the church, crossing themselves, bowing and kissing the icon. Others, standing in corners or along the walls, are reading prayer books to themselves.

Children stand quietly with their parents. Some may wander around, enchanted by the colors and the candle flames. Still others grow weary and sit on the floor at their mother's feet, or on a chair or bench set up along the back wall, perhaps next to their grandmother. Toleration of children's foibles is the rule; it is only when a child disturbs the service with noise or unacceptable behavior that he or she is taken out of the church. Interestingly enough, however, even at an early age, most of the children show a very high level of respect for the mysteries unfolding around them. As the service progresses, the royal doors open. Now all wandering ceases. All eyes are on the priest as he exits the altar and rejoins his congregation. What is completely absent, even at the most sacred moments of the liturgy, is the sense of a theatrical presentation, performed by the clergy and observed by the laity. Instead, the service offers a sense of mutual participation, of oneness, of community. At times there is an almost Edenic state of unity. There is no alienation here but instead a feeling of belonging. Indeed, for countless Christians around the world, to worship in an Orthodox church is to have come home at last.

Since my visit to St. Vladimir's Cathedral, I have tried to compare the worship experience there with that of many of the other churches I have attended. Few have come close. Sermons can be inspiring, corrective, and even life-changing. The reading of Holy Scripture is always illuminating. But only once do I recall feeling profoundly lifted up into another realm during a Protestant worship service.

The occasion took place in John Wimber's church—the original Vineyard Christian Fellowship in Southern California. It was a Sunday evening, and over a thousand people had gathered. During a time of praise and worship, we all were standing, singing song after song, and every voice was lost in the harmony, in the synergy.

135

Come let us worship and bow down. . . .
Allelulia, allelulia, allelulia. . . .

In that timeless moment, there was no self-conscious concern about vocal excellence. No talk of denominational disagreement. No exclusion of anyone. There was nothing but the song, its spirit of praise, its nearly overpowering intensity. That worship service, like the one at St. Vladimir's, was for me a brief glimpse of St. John's vision in the Revelation, the kingdom "on earth as it is in heaven."

It seemed, for a little while, that every creature in that auditorium was singing in harmony with every creature in the heavenly host. There were not many voices but one. There were not many songs but a single hymn. There were not many forms of worship but one true and transformative expression: the losing of the human creature in the presence of the holy Creator.

Years later, I became acquainted with the ancient words of the Divine Liturgy, as sung in the Orthodox church. As the priest dismisses the people, his words are a fitting blessing in every church, in every corner of the world, in the midst of every Christian confession. They apply to all who name the Name; to every soul that worships God, through Christ, in spirit and in truth:

*Lord, bless those who praise You
and sanctify those who trust in You.
Save Your people and bless Your inheritance.
Protect the whole body of Your Church.
Sanctify those who love the beauty of Your house.
Glorify them in return by Your divine Power,
and do not forsake us who hope in You.*

Grant peace to Your world,
to your churches, to the clergy. . . . and to all Your
    people.
For every good and perfect gift is from above,
Coming from You, the Father of lights.
To You we give glory, thanksgiving and worship,
To the Father and the Son and the Holy Spirit,
Now and forever and to the ages of ages.
Amen.

Notes

. . . *God enters into our three-dimensional world.* G. M. Prokhorov, F. von Lilienfeld, S. S. Bychkov, "Pamiati Otsa Ionna Meyendorfa," in *Mera*, vol. 2 (St. Petersburg: Glagol Press, 1993), 13, here translated by Elizabeth Zelensky.

. . . *humankind's thirst for something beyond.* Archimandrite Vasileos, *Hymn of Entry,* (Crestwood, NY: St. Vladimir's Seminary Press, 1984), 81.

. . . *moment in the church service.* Leonid Ouspensky and Vladimir Lossky, *The Meaning of Icons,* tr. G. E. H. Palmer and E. Kadlouhsky (Crestwood, NY: St. Vladimir's Seminary Press, 1983), 59.

Epilogue

Just as we are responsible for what we eat, so we are responsible
for what we see. It is easy to become a victim of the vast array of
visual stimuli surrounding us. The "powers and principalities"
control many of our daily images. Posters, billboards, television,
videocassettes, movies and store windows continuously assault our
eyes and inscribe their images upon our memories.

Still we do not have to be passive victims of a world that wants
to entertain and distract us. We can make some decisions and
choices. A spiritual life in the midst of our energy-draining society
requires us to take conscious steps to safeguard that inner space
where we can keep our eyes fixed on the beauty of the Lord.

—Henri Nouwen, *Behold the Beauty of the Lord*

Why would a Western Christian choose to contemplate Eastern
Orthodox icons? At first glance, the possibility of finding
modern-day value in such an ancient form of communication may
seem unlikely. It could be said that the appreciation of icons is an

acquired taste. Yet twenty-first century believers are increasingly fascinated by icons and are drawn to them, not only visiting them in museums and art collections but introducing icons into their lives and using them devotionally as aids to a deeper spiritual life.

We believe there are at least three reasons for this. First, as Henri Nouwen says, we are bombarded by images of every kind—violent, profane, manipulative, fearful, and seductive. When we have a choice about what we take into our minds visually, as he suggests, we are wise "to take conscious steps to safeguard" our inner lives by selecting imagery that expresses beauty, truth, and goodness.

Icons are not simply paintings that have come from artists' creative imagination and technical skills. As we've seen, they are written in an ancient and holy language of color and symbolism. The iconographic tradition brings more than form and color to us; it also brings subtler messages. Some people, for example, describe feelings of peace or tranquility after sitting quietly with Rublev's Holy Trinity icon. Others express an awareness of God's tender mercies in the presence of the Vladimir Theotokos. These responses are not intellectual or academic, although they may lead the mind to conscious reflection. They are intuitive responses that bypass the familiar media of text and spoken word.

That brings us to a second reason for contemplating icons. Icons can speak directly to the heart, and they communicate the great realities of truth, beauty, and goodness. We believe these realities are universal and transcendent and relate to one another in a profound way. Icons help us think about their status—an ever-diminishing status, it might seem—in our post-modern society.

Truth, as an objective reality, is sometimes blurred by relativism and subjective reactions: "My truth is not necessarily your truth." It has become unfashionable in some circles to imply that absolute truth even exists. Meanwhile, as we look around at such things as fashion, film, and fine art, we may notice that beauty, like truth, seems to have been devalued as well. Could this have happened because beauty and truth are irrevocably linked? Emily Dickenson expresses the relationship between these two values:

> I died for Beauty—but was scarce
> Adjusted in the tomb
> When one who died for Truth was lain
> In an adjoining room.
>
> He questioned softly why I failed?
> "For Beauty," I replied.
> "And I for Truth—themself are one—
> We brethren are," he said.
>
> And so, as kinsman met a night,
> We talked between the rooms,
> Until the moss had reached our lips,
> And covered up our names.

If the beauty of icons reflects truth—in the view of the Orthodox, the gospel truth—icons can also be said to inspire the third great value, goodness. The three great values are founded in and unified by the greatest of all ideals, love. And the message of the Christian gospel is, of course, love—love for God and love for fellow humans. Icons silently proclaim Jesus' two great commandments (Matt. 22:35–39). Perhaps they can break through the distractions that surround us and imprint his principles, and even his presence, on our inner lives.

Those distractions—and this brings us to the third reason for cherishing icons—are not only visual. A cacophony of noises and voices competing with one another pounds our ears as a soundtrack for the many stresses of daily living. Nearly everyone longs for peace and quiet, and people turn to various means of quieting themselves, including myriad forms of meditation and medication.

141

The Orthodox have long appreciated the deep value of contemplation and the balance it brings to everyday life. To sit with an icon silently, to allow it to speak its language to the soul and spirit, is to enter a place of retreat. It is to choose not only a visual image but an unspoken message about eternity. It is to glimpse, through a heavenly window, into a world where truth, beauty, and goodness shine like the sun, where the air is full of peace, and where the love of Christ reigns over all.